GCSEs in 2021
The Complete Guide

2021. What a time to be in Year 11...

What can we say? We know everything's been turned upside down during your GCSEs, but this CGP book will help you come through it with the best grades possible.

It's packed with expert advice on how to stay upbeat and keep learning effectively — plus super-useful planners that'll turn you into a master of time management.

There's even a free Online Edition of the whole book, so you can look up some cheeky study tips wherever you have internet connection. All right, 2021. Let's do this.

How to access your free Online Edition

This book includes a free Online Edition to read on your PC, Mac or tablet. You'll just need to go to **cgpbooks.co.uk/extras** and enter this code:

0964 7978 6568 1883

By the way, this code only works for one person. If somebody else has used this book before you, they might have already claimed the Online Edition.

Contents

GCSEs in 2021

Making a Start

Looking After Yourself

Revision Techniques

Tests and Assessments

Know Your Subject

Your Study Planner

Published by CGP

Editors: Tom Carney, Andy Cashmore, Heather Cowley, Rachel Craig-McFeely, Gabrielle Richardson, Sean Walsh

Contributors: Ben Armstrong, Graham Fletcher, Paddy Gannon, Steve Gough, David Martindill, Deanne Morris, Steve Stoddard, Sue Todd, Ben Wallace

With thanks to Matt Topping for the proofreading. With thanks to Lottie Edwards for the copyright research.

ISBN: 978 1 78908 757 4
Printed by Elanders Ltd, Newcastle upon Tyne.

Clipart from Corel®
Based on the classic CGP style created by Richard Parsons.

How to Use this Book

Due to coronavirus, GCSEs will be a little bit different compared to previous years — but don't worry, like a good blanket this book has you covered. Grab yourself a cup of tea and a biscuit, then dive right in...

GCSEs are Being Assessed Differently This Year*

1) All formal GCSE exams in the summer of 2021 have been cancelled.
2) Exam results will be replaced by grades decided by your teachers.
3) Teachers will base your grades on a range of evidence including mock exams, class tests, essays and your work throughout the course.

Unlike in 2020, there won't be an algorithm involved in grades this year.

Read the First Half of this Book for Advice

The first half of this book gives you guidance and strategies on how best to study in 2021:

Use the Second Half to Plan Your Work

1) At the back of this book are a planner for important dates, topic planners and study planners for you to fill in.
2) There's also step-by-step information on how to plan your work so you use your time wisely.
3) Once you've read the book and filled in your study planner, you'll be ready to begin studying.

*All information in this book correct at the time of printing.

What to Expect — and When

No one knows the future — except my cat. Here's a run down of what to expect for your GCSEs this summer.

Exams have been Replaced by Teachers' Grades

What Normally Happens:
- Exam boards set compulsory exams for each subject.
- Exams take place between May and June.
- Pupils go on study leave.
- Some subjects also have non-exam assessments.
- Results are published in late August.

How 2021 is Different
- There will be no official GCSE exams in 2021. Instead you will be given grades by your teachers based on a range of evidence.
- Exam boards are putting together questions that teachers may set to help them decide on your grades. These could be exam-style questions, and will be on topics that you have studied — see the next page for more details.
- Your teacher will also look at other work you do in class, such as topic tests, essays or other assignments.
- They'll bear in mind your school work throughout the course, particularly work done in the spring and summer terms of Year 11.
- Non-exam assessments will go ahead, but you will not be disadvantaged if you cannot complete them.
- Because of disruptions to learning, you may not get study leave — you will need to fit your revision around your lessons.
- You'll get your grades on August 12th 2021.

Private Candidates Will Be Assessed in a Similar Way

1) **If you're a private candidate (e.g. you are home-schooled), your grades will also be decided by teachers instead of formal exams.**
2) **You'll need to set this up yourself — e.g. your parents should contact a school that teaches the subjects you are studying.**
3) **You will have to give an examination centre a range of evidence for your abilities — e.g. you could take some exam-style questions provided by exam boards, as well as submitting examples of work you've completed throughout the year. You'll only be assessed on topics that you've studied.**

Your examination centre will give more detail about how they will assess you.

I had Great Expectations for my test, but all the questions were on Frankenstein...

This year is a bit strange and uncertain, but one way to feel more in control is to make sure you know how your GCSEs are going to be assessed — that way you can prepare yourself effectively and avoid any nasty surprises.

Questions from the Exam Boards

'Questions from the exam boards' isn't exactly the most catchy name, but it does what it says on the tin — to decide your grade, your teacher might set you some questions which are written by exam boards. Told you.

The Exam Boards will set Some Questions

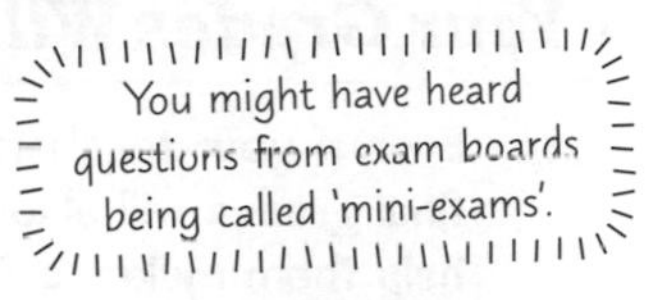

1) Your school might decide to set questions written by the exam boards.
2) The questions will be similar to, or even the same as, ones in past papers — so it's really important to practise past paper questions (see p.30). However, not all the questions will be from previous papers, so don't rely on just memorising past paper answers.
3) Your answers will be marked by your teachers rather than examiners.
4) Your teachers will look at your results alongside your work throughout the course and other non-exam assessments to help them decide which final grades to give you (see next page).

These Questions will Let You Show Your Skills

1) Questions from exam boards haven't been created to make your life a misery — they're actually a great way to show what you can do and demonstrate everything you've learnt in the last two years.
2) You might have missed some lessons because of school disruption, having to self-isolate or even being ill — the range of questions are designed to take into account this disturbance to your learning:

Don't worry, you won't have to answer a full paper of questions covering the entire GCSE specification — your teachers will be able to choose which topics you need to answer questions on so that you can focus your revision.

There's No Set Exam Timetable

1) You might be set some questions from exam boards any time between the end of March and June 18th — your teachers will tell you nearer the time.
2) It will be up to your school where you do these questions — you'll probably take them in class, but if you're self-isolating you may be able to do them at home.
3) Your teacher will decide how long you'll have to answer the questions and whether you'll need to take them under exam conditions.

Guitar-playing during tests is still not encouraged.

Exam boards, exam bored...

...but there's nothing like a test to liven up your day. Even though answering questions from exam boards isn't a formal exam, it's still important to take them seriously — they could play a key role in deciding your overall grades.

How Else Teachers Will Decide Grades

As promised, here's some more detail on the kinds of things teachers will use to decide your grades.

Your Grades Will Be Based on a Wide Range of Evidence

ASK YOUR TEACHER

1) Even if your teachers choose to use questions set by the exam boards, your final grades will also take into account a wide range of evidence — this is to help them make as fair a representation of your abilities as possible.
2) There are several things your teachers could take into account:

Your school should tell you how each of your subjects will be assessed.

Class Tests

- Teachers are allowed to design their own tests instead of using questions created by the exam boards.
- These tests might be end-of-topic tests or essay questions based on topics you've already covered in class.

Mock Exam Results

- If you've already done a mock exam (or your teacher sets one), this could be used to help decide your final grade.

Work Throughout the Year

- Your work across the course could be used to decide your final grade, particularly work done towards the end of this year.
- Don't worry — your teacher will consider any disruptions to your learning.

See p.26-37 for in-depth information on teacher and non-exam assessments.

Some Subjects Have Non-Exam Assessments

1) Some subjects are usually assessed by a combination of exam and non-exam assessments, e.g. Drama.
2) You won't be disadvantaged if you haven't been able to do your non-exam assessment — your grade will be weighted towards any work that you have been able to complete.
3) For subjects that are only examined by non-exam assessments, e.g. Art and Design, your grade will be based entirely on your portfolio.
4) You won't be marked down if you haven't been able to complete your portfolio — e.g. if you haven't been able to make your final piece, your teacher will assess your designs and any mock-ups you have made.

You may be allowed to complete your non-exam assessments at home — but you must not receive any help and you will have to prove the work is your own.

Rock, paper, scissors...

Your teachers won't decide your grade at random — they have to be able to prove that you got the result you deserved. It's actually quite a bit of pressure, but you can make their decision easier by smashing your assessments.

What To Do If You Don't Get the Grades You Want

Your teacher will have worked hard to assess your work and give you the grade you deserve. Sadly, not everyone can get the top grades, but there are things you can do if you feel like your grade isn't fair.

You Could Appeal Your Grade

In August, if you're not happy that your grade reflects your abilities, you could decide to appeal your grade — here's how it works:

Horatio wouldn't settle for anything less than a grade 10.

1) When they are deciding your grade, your teacher will be required to provide evidence for their decision.
2) You can appeal to your school — they will check whether an administrative error was made when deciding your grade.
3) Your grade could be adjusted if your school finds there was an error.
4) However, if you're still not happy with your grade, you can ask your school to appeal to the exam board. They will review your teacher's evidence for your result to check that the grade awarded was fair.
5) Bear in mind that when you appeal your grade to your school or exam board, it might go up or down.

There Should be an Opportunity to Sit Exams in the Autumn

1) **If your result hasn't improved after appealing it, you might want to sit an exam for that subject to get a better grade.**
2) **The government has said that there should be exams for all GCSE subjects in autumn 2021 — this means that you shouldn't have to wait a whole year to improve your grade.**
3) **The timetable for these exams should be released later this year.**

Things to Consider about these Exams...

- **Talk to your subject teacher to see whether they think you could achieve a higher grade.**
- **Think about how you will fit these exams around your other work — if you're starting college in the autumn, taking GCSE exams could put you under lots of extra pressure.**
- **Consider whether it's worth it — even if your grades were lower than you wanted, if you already have a place at college or on an apprenticeship it might not be worth taking them.**

Getting a grade 9 sounds pretty appealing...

Sadly, you can't just ask for a grade 9 — but if you don't get the results you expected, you can do something about it. Personally I would challenge my teacher to a three-legged race, but appealing your grade works too.

What To Do First

You're probably wondering how to get started with preparing for your assessments. Something we're certain about is that knowing what you'll be assessed on is key — that, and the fact I won't let my sister cut my hair...

Find Out What You Could Be Tested On

1) The pandemic has affected how GCSEs have been taught this year, so you might not have covered everything on the specification.
2) Don't worry — your teachers will take this into account when they're planning how to assess your work and award your grade.
3) It's important to find out exactly what you could be assessed on, so make sure you speak to your teachers to find out the details.
4) They'll be able to tell you which topics you need to know for your assessments and if there are any areas you don't need to worry about.

Don't Panic If You Need To Catch Up On Topics

1) If you've missed classes due to self-isolation, health reasons or not having access to online lessons, try to catch up.
2) Make a plan for what you can realistically learn in the time you have.

You could use the study planners at the back of this book to help you plan your work (see p.72-85).

Learning things on your own can be tricky, but fear not — there are some great tips on pages 10-12 to help you get to grips with it.

Think About What To Prioritise

There are some things you can do to help you decide what to focus on first:

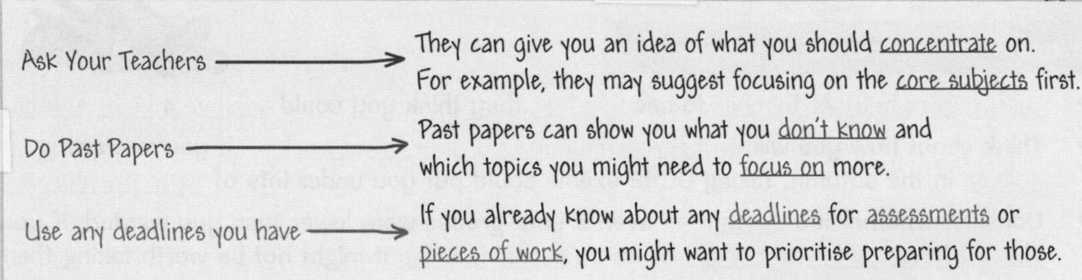

Focus on the important things — no not cake (well maybe a little)...

Studying can seem overwhelming at the best of times, so it's a good idea to take it one step at a time. Decide on the best areas to focus on first — it'll give you a good start towards your preparation and get you on the right track.

Organisation and Planning

Some things are best when you dive straight in — preparing for assessments is not one of those things. Making a plan means you can spend more time working and less time worrying you've forgotten something.

Planning Will Make You Feel in Control

Spend time on a solid plan, but don't spend so long that you don't have time to work.

Reasons to Plan

- It gives you the best chance to cover everything you need to
- You won't forget any topics
- You can prioritise tricky subjects
- It reduces stress
- It's more efficient

Check what you need to work on with your teachers.

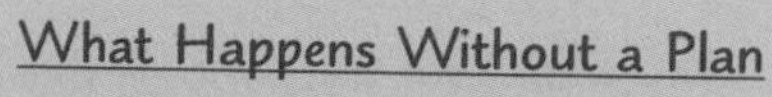

- You'll waste time deciding what to work on in each session
- You might not allow enough time to work on everything
- You can't easily check what you've already worked on
- You may forget some topics

Timetables Can Help You Plan

A topic and study planner will help you schedule your work and see how you're progressing. You can find handy versions ready to fill in at the back of this book on pages 60-85.

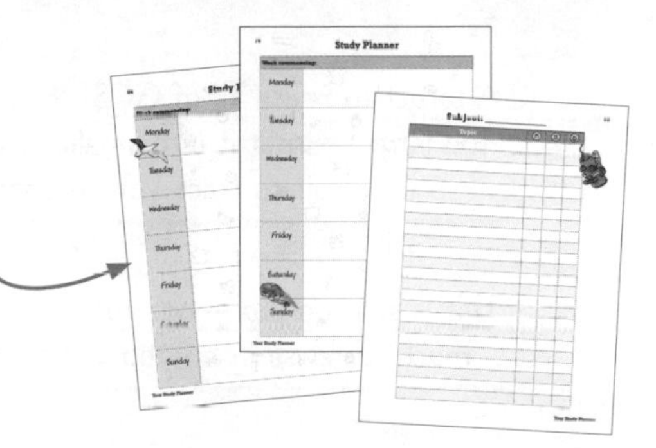

Being Organised Will Save Time

1) **Organise your notes and books for each subject to make it easier to find information.**
2) **Write a to-do list, then prioritise which tasks need to be done first — completing tasks on a to-do list can make you feel good.**
3) **Make sure you have all the stationery you need (lots of paper, pens, a calculator etc.) so you can crack on with your work without a fuss.**

To-Do List

1 • Buy pens and a new protractor
3 • Tidy desk
2 • Make a timetable
4 • Organise Physics notes folder
5 • Write the most hilarious side-splitting joke to round off the 'Organisation and Planning' page.

Did you hear the one about

Planning all your work will help you remember to get every little last thing done. Eventually...

Setting Targets

Knowing what you want to achieve over the next few months will help you stay on track. It's important to keep your overall targets in mind, but focusing on the smaller steps you can take each day will help you reach them.

Make Realistic Targets in a Sensible Time Frame

1) **Setting a time frame to achieve your targets helps with motivation.**
2) **You need to be realistic though. For example:**

- **Two weeks for fractions — this is too long on a small topic.**
- **An hour for all of chemistry — you'll either have too little time or rush through it.**

3) **Generally, it's better to give yourself slightly more time than you think you'll need.**
4) **It's much easier to work towards and achieve small targets — to do this, you'll need to work out how to break down a bigger goal:**

You'll need to consider any classwork or homework you have when setting time frames — it's important to keep up with these as well as revising.

EXAMPLE:

Imagine your goal is to revise everything you need for your GCSE History assessment(s). Here's how you could set targets for your revision sessions:

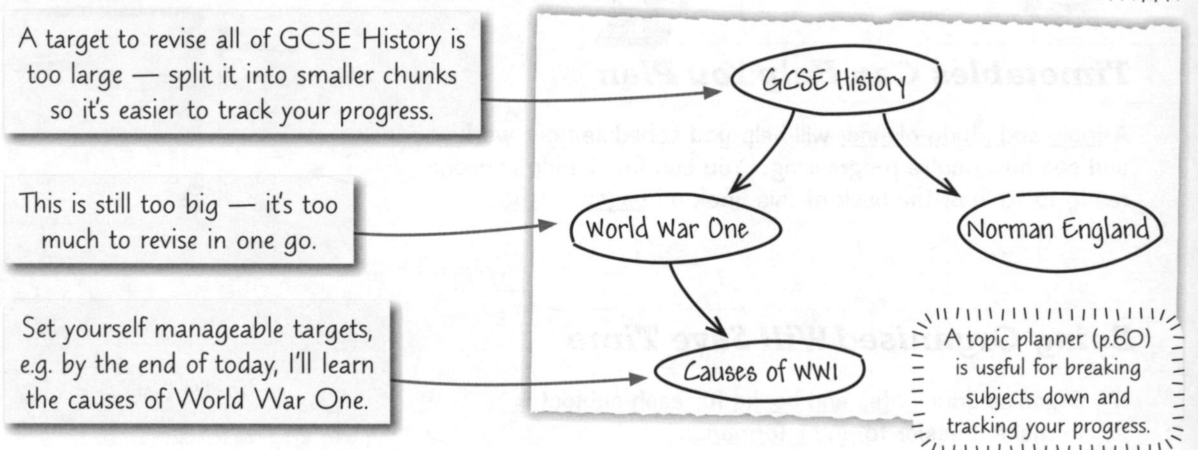

A topic planner (p.60) is useful for breaking subjects down and tracking your progress.

Reward Yourself For Hitting Targets

1) **It's been a very tough year, so make sure you reward yourself for hitting targets.**
2) **You might plan a reward for finishing a tricky topic or a set of practice questions.**
3) **Your rewards should be simple and help you relax — e.g. some TV or a walk.**
4) **Plan a bigger treat for after your assessments as something to look forward to.**

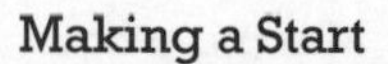

Motivation

You may not always feel like studying, but thinking about how it will help with your goals can motivate you.

Knowing Why You're Working Hard Can Motivate You

1) Think about why you want to be successful in your GCSEs. It may be:
   - to prepare yourself for what you're doing next year e.g. going to sixth form or college
   - to help you one day get your dream job
   - to prove to yourself and others that you can do it
2) Be positive about what you can achieve in the time you have.
3) Focus on your goals and don't compare yourself to other people. This can help keep you positive in a tough year.

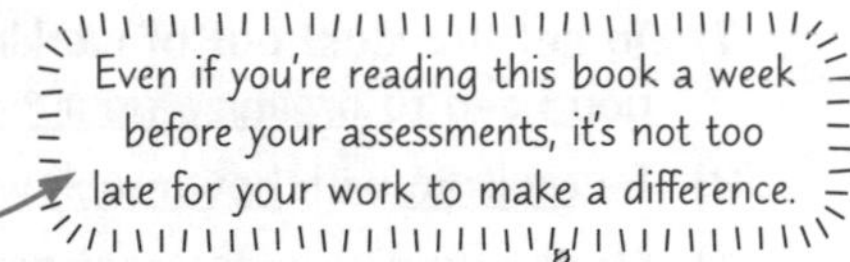

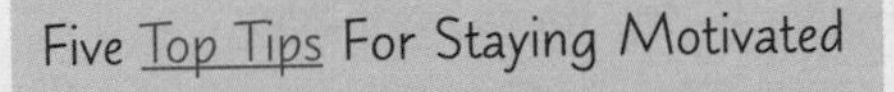

1. Set small targets with rewards (see p.8).
2. Remind yourself of your long-term goals.
3. Plan a big treat for after your assessments.
4. Use a topic planner so you can see the progress you've made.
5. If you're dreading a particular topic, start with some easier topics first.

Don't Waste Valuable Time

1) With all that's going on in the world, you might feel overwhelmed — but it's important to not put off things that need doing and to make the most of your working time.
2) Here are some things you can do to help:
   - Turn off your phone, Netflix and other distractions.
   - Give yourself regular breaks — it'll help you keep focused when you're working.
   - Break up your work into small chunks so it's not one endless slog.
   - Start with something small — this will ease you into focusing on your work.

This climb takes the biscuit...

You can't say "I can't" without saying "I can"...

If you ever find yourself completely unmotivated, try doing something short and active that can clear your mind. I'm a big fan of kitchen dance parties, running around the block in 80s sportswear and mastering the worm.

Filling in the Gaps

It's likely that you'll have missed some lessons this year, so you may need to fill in the gaps in your knowledge. This will require a bit of independent work on your part, which is where this page comes in handy.

Independent Work Requires Organisation

1) **Independent study involves getting to grips with the subject content in your own time.**
2) **To get the most out of working independently, you need to organise your time effectively.**
3) **Be realistic with how much work you can get done (see p.8).**
4) **Make effective notes that can help you when you revise (see p.11).**

Learning to work independently is something that will be really useful if you go on to do further study.

There Are Various Ways Of Filling In The Gaps

Catching up on work doesn't just mean reading textbooks — try these methods:

Ask for class notes

- For lessons you missed, ask your teacher if they have any notes or presentations you could look at.
- Use these to make your own set of notes (see p.11) — this will make the information easier to understand and help you remember it better.

Do your own research

- Read books or revision guides and make your own notes.
- Find things you could watch or listen to that are useful for your subjects, e.g. videos of science practicals you haven't been able to do.
- You could check websites that have GCSE-level information.

Once you've filled in the gaps, you need to consolidate your new-found knowledge — here are some ideas:

Work with friends and family

- Read through notes with a friend or test each other on material you've learnt, e.g. definitions or formulas.
- Do presentations or hold mock debates to help you develop ideas and arguments.
- You could also ask someone in your house to test you on topics, or explain to them a topic you've learnt to make sure you understand it.

Practise what you've learnt

- Test yourself using worksheets from your teacher or CGP workbooks — make sure you have the answers so you can check how well you understand everything.
- For topics you struggled on, go back and research those areas a bit more.

Cement won't help you fill in these gaps...

Filling in the gaps in your knowledge and working independently can be a challenge, but learning how to do them will build vital skills. Think about studying like building a house — no one wants a house with holes in it. Brrr.

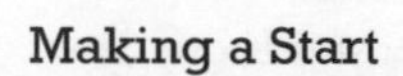

Making Notes

Making effective notes will help you to fill any gaps in your knowledge. It's important that your notes are as useful as possible because you'll want to refer back to them when you start going back over topics.

Making Notes Should Be An Active Process

1) Writing notes is about more than just copying things down word for word.
2) Instead, you should write the key information in your own words. This will help you actively learn the content while you're studying.
3) It will also make your notes easier to understand and to refer to.
4) Make sure your notes include all the information you need to know (see p.6), but nothing extra. There's no point in writing down anything you won't be assessed on.

Make Sure Your Notes Are Clear

Use a mixture of techniques to draw attention to key information in your notes:

- Add subheadings to your notes to organise the information.
- Use highlighting to pick out the most important points.
- Colour-code information to show links, e.g. write all definitions in orange.

Here's how you could write up notes about *The Merchant of Venice* for GCSE English.

Theme: Prejudice

You don't need to write in full sentences — just make sure your notes are clear.

Characters who are victims of prejudice:

- Shylock — Christian characters are hostile towards him. Duke calls him "inhuman wretch".
- Jessica — Experiences anti-Semitism, even after marrying Lorenzo and becoming Christian.

Characters who are prejudiced:

- Antonio — He is anti-Semitic and would "spit on" Shylock.
- Shylock — Hates Antonio "for he is a Christian".
- Portia — Makes racist remark about Prince of Morocco's "complexion".
  — Makes stereotypical comments about nationality of her suitors.

I made some notes on map reading, but I seem to have lost them...

You won't have a great deal of time to look back over your notes, so it's important that they're as clear as possible. If you're short on time, ask your teacher which topics you should focus on — and keep them away from your dog.

Focus On How You Work Best

There's no one 'right' way to learn or revise, but there are some common learning styles people find useful. This page should give you some ideas for how you could approach your study or revision time.

There Are Four Main Learning Styles

1) **Most people identify with one or two of these learning styles more than the others.**
2) **You might benefit from using a mixture of styles — it'll add variety to your time spent studying.**

- Some people prefer learning visually — they learn best by using diagrams and graphic representations.
- Useful learning techniques include making flash cards or mind maps, colour-coding notes and illustrating material with pictures or diagrams.

- Some people work best aurally — they learn by speaking and listening.
- Helpful learning techniques include reading material out loud, listening to podcasts on course topics, making up mnemonics and discussing topics with friends.

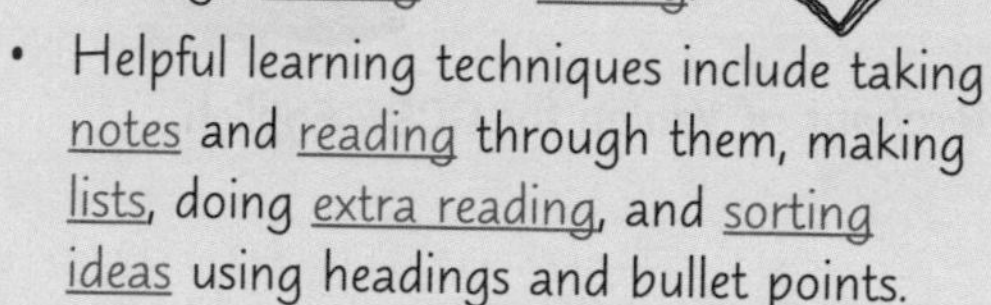

- Some people learn best through reading and writing.
- Helpful learning techniques include taking notes and reading through them, making lists, doing extra reading, and sorting ideas using headings and bullet points.

- Some people prefer learning physically — they learn best by doing things, such as activities.
- Useful learning techniques include incorporating real-world examples into notes and finding ways to include physical activity when you study (e.g. taking a walk).

3) **There's more about the different techniques you could use for study and revision on pages 19-25.**

Make The Most of Your Study Time

Try these ideas for size if you're looking for ways to help you concentrate and learn more effectively:

1) **Some people find music helps them study — you could also try nature sounds or white noise.**
2) **Find out whether you work best in big chunks (50 minutes) or small chunks (25 minutes).**
3) **You can do things to adapt your study environment for working (see page 13).**
4) **Dressing smartly can get you into the right mindset to work — go full suit and tie if it helps.**

My learning style involves wearing sunglasses and a baseball cap...

Learning styles aren't an exact science, but thinking about how you might learn best will help you to organise your study time. Focusing on techniques that you find most useful will also help you study more effectively.

Your Study Environment

To be productive, it's important to create a study environment you can work well in. For example, the gymnast in your class might find it easier to work in a completely different way to you...

Make Your Home Study Space Work for You

Studying at home can be difficult — you may get distracted by your family, or you may be fed up of spending so much time there. However, there are things you can do to make studying at home work for you:

1) **If you have to work in your bedroom, try to avoid studying on your bed so that you don't start to associate it with work — this could affect your sleep.**
2) **Try to set up a study space in a quiet part of the house. Shut the door for some privacy, and set up your study space as you want.**
3) **If you have to work in a room with other members of your family, put in some headphones and try listening to music or white noise to block out any distractions.**

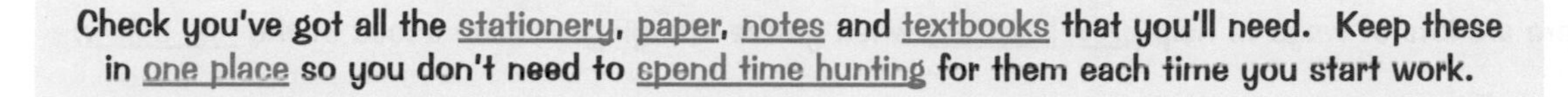

Check you've got all the stationery, paper, notes and textbooks that you'll need. Keep these in one place so you don't need to spend time hunting for them each time you start work.

A Tidy Study Space is Important

It's easier to work if your study space is tidy.
Here's one we made earlier:

Even if you've spent a lot of time studying at home during the pandemic, moving some furniture or tidying up can help the space feel fresh again.

My astronaut friend loves this page on study spaces...

Piles of books and folders make it hard to get to notes quickly — if you can, use a bookshelf to keep them tidy and accessible. Also avoid clutter and rubbish on your desk, as important things can get lost when everything is on top of each other.

Looking After Your Mental Health

These pages have loads of self-care tips to help you avoid feeling too stressed, tired or overworked.

It has been a Stressful Year

1) The last year has been difficult — and with GCSE pressure on top of a global pandemic, it's easy to feel overwhelmed.
2) You won't be alone in feeling under pressure — it's likely your classmates are also finding this time stressful.
3) It can really help to talk to someone if you're feeling overwhelmed — see p.15.

Signs of Stress include:

- A loss of appetite
- Feeling emotional
- Feeling anxious
- Difficulty concentrating
- Struggling to sleep
- Sudden weight change

Keep your Mental Health in Mind

There are lots of ways to help prevent stress when you're studying — have a look at the tips below:

Celebrate small wins — acknowledging the progress you've made will help you stay motivated. E.g. you could write down one thing every day that you're proud of achieving in your work.

Make sure your targets for each day are realistic — working in small, manageable chunks will help you stay positive.

Take breaks — this will help you relax and make your studying or revision more effective.

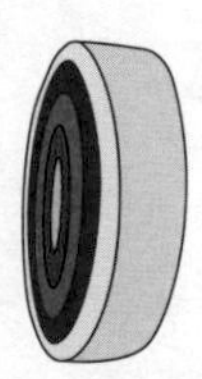

Make sure you leave some of your evening free to relax — working too late into the evening can affect your sleep (see page 18).

Don't compare yourself to others — everyone works in different ways, so just focus on what you're managing to do each day.

Don't worry if you're not able to stick to your schedule 100% of the time — there's a lot going on and it's important to look after yourself.

If you're struggling to stay on track, it might be worth rethinking your schedule to make it work better for you.

Treat yourself if you're studying a tricky topic — this will help you feel motivated (see page 8).

Looking After Your Mental Health

Take a Break from Technology

1) In the last year, you've probably spent a lot of time staring at a screen — they're used more than ever for work, socialising and relaxation.
2) However, it's important to give yourself a break from technology — too much screen-time can strain your eyes and affect your sleep.
3) Even just spending some time away from your screen or study area can help — for example:
   - Try taking breaks which don't involve watching TV or scrolling through social media.
   - Eat meals away from your study space and screen.
4) Try to set aside time every day to go outside and get some fresh air.

Even if you're not working at a screen, it's still important to take breaks from studying to avoid getting a sore back or neck.

It can be Helpful to Talk to People

1) If you ever feel too stressed (about studying or anything else) remember that you're not alone — talking to someone about how you feel can help you share your anxieties and feel less worried.
2) You could talk to someone you trust — e.g. friends, family, teachers or your GP.
3) Arrange a call with a friend and let them know how you're doing — they might also be feeling anxious, so chatting can help you both support each other.
4) If you don't feel comfortable talking to someone you know, there are support services and helplines available where you can talk to someone confidentially.

- Try not to only contact friends through social media — it's good to talk to people face to face when possible, or on a call.
- Don't feel like you have to discuss studying with friends if it makes you feel worse.

Here are some helplines you could call or text:

Childline	Mind	Shout 85258
Call 0800 1111	Call 0300 123 3393	Text 'SHOUT' to 85258

Bottling up your stress won't help — tell people how you feel...

Studying is important, but it's not worth affecting your health. Make sure you take time out from working to do things you enjoy — not only will this make you happier, it'll also make studying easier.

Exercise

It's important for your physical *and* mental health to get up and move around rather than sitting down all day. You don't have to run a marathon — fitting exercise into your schedule can be a walk in the park (literally).

Exercise can Reduce Stress

1) Exercise reduces levels of your body's stress hormones, e.g. adrenaline.
2) It also stimulates the production of endorphins (chemicals in your brain that help you feel good). This can help you feel more energised and positive.
3) Exercising can take your mind off things you're worried about.
4) Taking time to exercise can help break up studying and give order to your day.
5) It can also be a way to socialise — e.g. if restrictions allow, you could go on a walk with a friend.

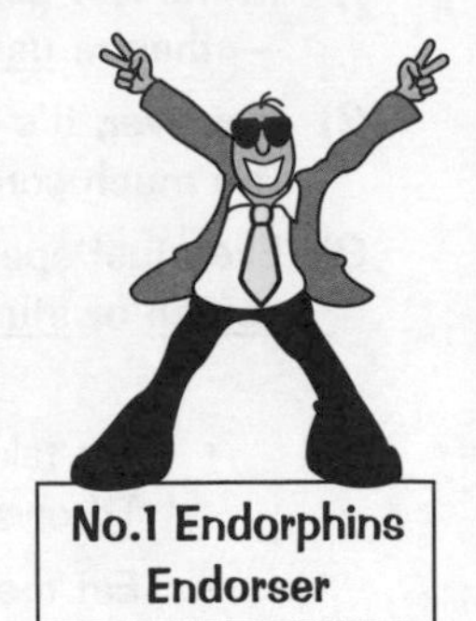

No.1 Endorphins Endorser

There are Lots of Ways to Exercise

If you don't enjoy running, don't force yourself to do it — do something that you enjoy and will feel motivated to do regularly. Here are some ideas:

Choose a kind of exercise that suits your fitness level and don't push yourself too far — it should be fun and relaxing.

Go outside

- Going for a walk, run or short bike ride in your local area is a great way to get some fresh air.
- You could exercise by yourself, or with a friend.
- Make sure you stick to government guidelines and social distancing when exercising outdoors.

Do an indoor workout

- Exercising at home is a great way to work out safely (and perfect if it's raining).
- There are loads of workouts to choose from online.
- Do a dance class, or try a HIIT (high-intensity interval training) workout — just make sure you have enough space to do so safely.

Try yoga or Pilates

- Yoga and Pilates combine exercise with breathing and meditation.
- There are lots of routines online which are easy to follow in your bedroom.
- They're a great way to stretch and relax — plus they can improve your focus and concentration.

Even if you don't want to do a full yoga routine, doing a few stretches can be a good break from work. Here are some examples — look them up online to see how to do them properly:

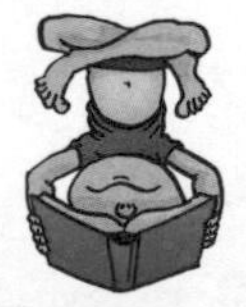

Child's pose

Downward facing dog

Cobra pose

Knot-a-pose

Mindfulness and Meditation

Practising mindfulness or meditation can help your brain switch off during breaks from studying. Ah, serenity.

Mindfulness means Paying Attention to the Present

1) Mindfulness is about taking the time to be aware of your thoughts and feelings, and to experience your different senses.
2) Practising mindfulness can help improve your mental well-being and make you feel more in control.
3) Mindfulness also gives your mind a break from studying and lets you come back to work feeling refreshed and calm.

Mindfulness techniques:

- Focus on the present — try to stop and appreciate small things as you go about your daily life, e.g. a bird singing on your walk.
- Do some breathing exercises — take several deep breaths in and out, focusing on the process of breathing. This will help de-clutter your brain.

Meditation can Help You Relax

1) Meditation can help you improve your concentration and reduce stress.
2) It's about focusing on something specific — e.g. your breathing, a positive word or an imagined scene. When your mind wanders to what you're having for dinner, train yourself to bring your thoughts back to your point of focus.
3) If you want to try some simple meditation, sit somewhere peaceful and free from distractions. Spend a few minutes taking deep breaths, focusing on your breathing.

There are Lots of Other Ways to Relax

- Listen to some music, or find a podcast about something that isn't related to studying.
- Spend time doing hobbies you enjoy at home — e.g. playing an instrument or reading.
- Work on a DIY project, or have a go at a new craft.
- Play a board game with your family (unless they're competitive, in which case probably avoid this — shouting isn't particularly relaxing.)
- Try out a new hobby — challenging yourself to do small things like cooking something new can help boost your self-confidence.
- Write a diary — this can help you unwind at the end of the day.

Take a deep breath in...

You might feel like you're too busy to meditate, but it's important to take breaks. Meditation may feel a bit silly at first, but even if it makes you laugh then that's a form of relaxation (unless it gives you hiccups). ***...and out.***

Sleep and Diet

Ah, my two favourite things in the world — snoozing and food. Getting a healthy amount of both these things will help to keep you in peak condition and make it easier to take in information. Yum.

1) Don't Skip Sleep to Do Work

Sleep helps you process what you've learnt.

2) Avoid Pricking Your Finger on a Spindle

Otherwise you'll sleep for a hundred years... wait, that's for a different book...

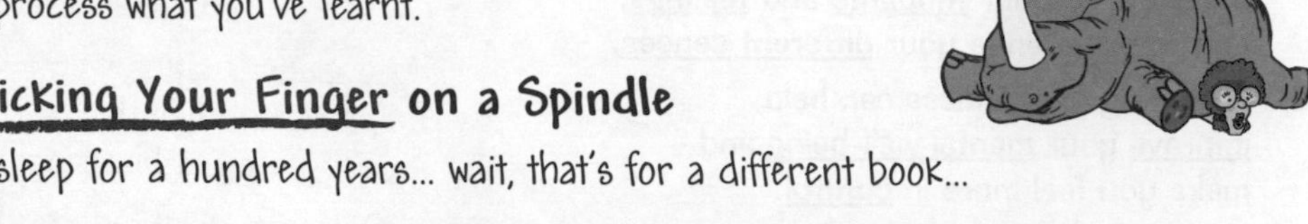

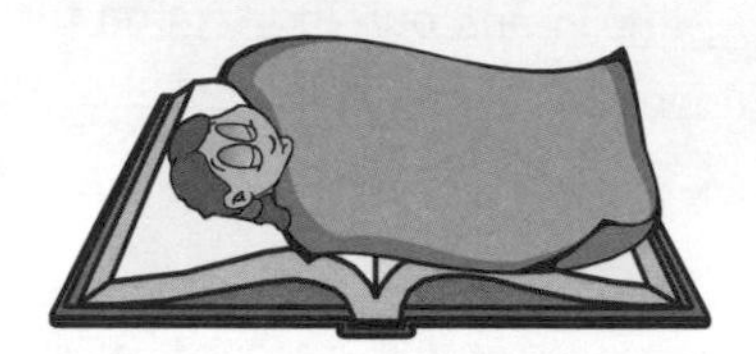

3) Do Something Relaxing Before Bed

Avoid caffeine, strenuous exercise and looking at your phone.

4) Sleep on Your Notes

You'll learn through osmosis. If you don't know what osmosis is, sleep on a biology book tonight...

5) Keep Your Phone Away From Your Bed

It'll disrupt your sleep if it keeps going off.

You best leaf right now, mate.

Meating you was a mistake.

6) Eat Plenty of Fruit and Veg

Yes, even broccoli (honestly, you grow to like it).

7) Don't Skip Meals

It makes it difficult to concentrate.

8) Get Plenty of Protein

Oily fish are great to eat (but hard to catch).

9) Only Have Sweets and Chocolate as an Occasional Treat

This was harder for me to write than it was for you to read.

10) Drink Lots of Water

From a glass, from a mug, from a bowl if you're a maverick.

"Snooze, glorious snooze..."

It is so, so important to look after yourself, especially during the double-whammy of a global pandemic and GCSEs. Making sure that you eat properly and get enough sleep is a key part of your self-care journey — you've got this.

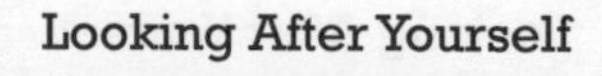

Learn, Revise, Test Yourself

Before jumping into revision, make sure you've understood the topic first. Read on my friend...

LEARN

The learning process starts in lessons and with assignments, but you might need to catch up on topics you missed (see p.10) or didn't understand first time around. Remember to check with your teacher whenever you're unsure about what to study.

It's really important to understand a topic before you start revising it. If there's anything you're not sure about, you could:

- look back over your notes carefully and read the textbook again.
- do some research online.
- ask your teacher.

ASK YOUR TEACHER

REVISE

When you're happy that you understand a topic, you can move on to revise it.

Revising is the process of going back over what you've learnt so that you're ready to answer questions on it.

There are many different ways to revise — here are just a few examples:

- condensing your notes (see p.20)
- mind maps (see p.21)
- flow charts (see p.22)
- flash cards (see p.23)

Try different techniques, then stick with the ones that work best for you — you'll need to use the time you have effectively, so don't waste time on techniques you don't find useful.

Don't worry if you find something you don't understand — just go back and learn it again.

To make a topic stick, test yourself on it at increasing intervals after revising it, e.g. after half an hour, after two hours, after a day etc.

TEST YOURSELF

Once you're happy that you know a topic, it's time to test yourself:

- You could start by doing some quick fact recall questions, and then go on to some practice exam questions.
- It's really important to do some realistic exam practice — some questions will ask you to apply what you've learnt in different ways so it's good to know you can do this. Check with your teacher about what you need to do.

If there's something you can't remember, go back to your notes and revise it again.

Condensing Your Notes

Now you know how to get started, it's time to get cracking. The first step is to get your notes into order — you can't learn every word you've ever written so you need to condense them. Here we go...

Start With Your Notes

Examples of each of these revision techniques can be found in the online edition — just scan this QR code or go to cgpbooks.co.uk/GCSE2021.

1) **You'll need to start off with some useful notes, including:**
   - **A CGP Revision Guide (the ideal revision companion, of course)**
   - **your class notes (there's more about writing notes on p.11)**
   - **text books**
   - **revision sheets from your teacher**

2) **Read over them and make sure you understand what you've read — simplifying a topic into key points won't help you if you don't understand your original notes.**

Condense Them In Your Own Words

1) **You'll want to simplify and summarise your notes into key points so they're easier to revise from.**
2) **Aim to get each topic onto a single page. Cut out the waffle and pick out what's important.**
3) **Try to reorganise the material in some way, e.g. by grouping it differently or linking topics together.**
4) **How you present your notes might depend on the subject. For example, you could make:**

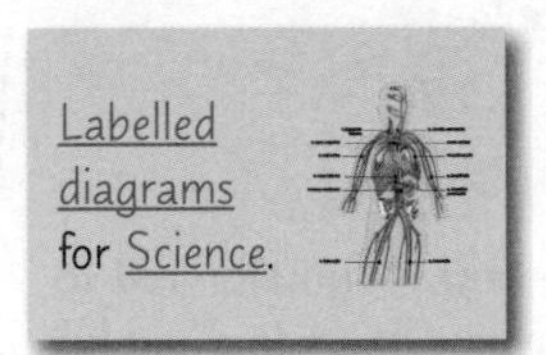

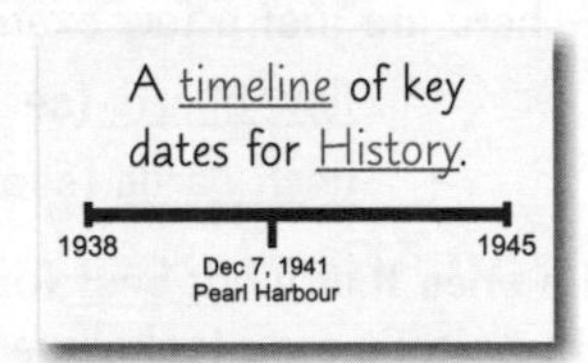

A table of formulas and rules for Maths.

$a^2 + b^2 = c^2$

5) **Condensing topics makes your revision interactive — it's better than just re-reading your notes again. Plus, you're more likely to remember your own words than something someone else has written*.**

Test Yourself On What You've Covered

It's a good idea to come back and test yourself again later, to see what you can still remember. (See more about spaced practice on p.56.)

When you've simplified a topic, it's time to test yourself:

1) **Cover up your notes and write down as much as you can remember.**
2) **Compare what you've written to your notes then fill in any gaps — use a different colour so you know which bits you missed.**
3) **Keep doing this until you remember everything on the topic.**

**apart from my words — you'll definitely remember my words...*

The key to condensing is to pick out the right points. If it helps, you might want to go through and highlight the important bits before you start writing. There's no 'right' way of doing it, just the way that works for you.

Drawing Mind Maps

If you say 'mind map' as fast as you can 40 times while looking at a topic, one will draw itself...

A Mind Map is a Type of Diagram

1) Mind maps are a visual way to organise information.
2) One mind map usually represents one topic.
3) The name of the topic goes in the middle, with sub-topics and further detail added around it.
4) Details are short and to the point.
5) Boxes or bubbles around some of the information can help it stand out.
6) A good mind map uses colour and images.

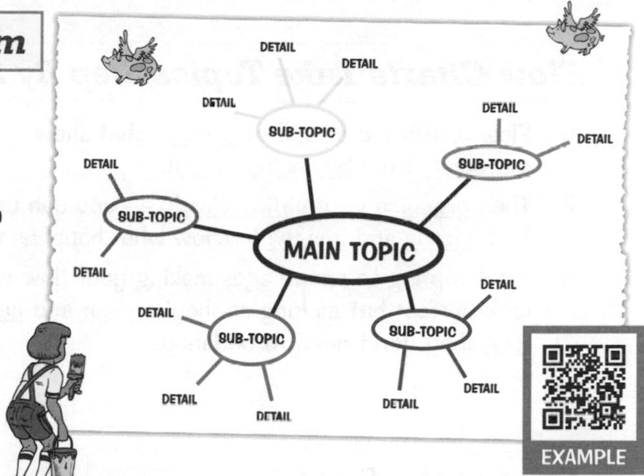

EXAMPLE

Mind Maps Are Great For Revising Topics

1) Organising material visually can make it easier to recall.
2) Colour and images can help topics and information to stick in your memory.
3) Mind maps can help you to identify the key ideas of a topic and find links between them, which can help you see the topic in different ways.

You Can Use Them Throughout Your Revision

Mind maps are really useful for subjects where there are lots of links between ideas (e.g. History or English) but less useful for learning a list of formulas or a vocab list.

At the start

Use your notes and other resources to draw a mind map of a topic — it's a great way of revising key information.

During revision

You could pin your completed mind maps up in your study space so that you see them regularly.

To test yourself

Draw a mind map of a topic from memory, then refer to the original and fill in any gaps in a different colour — this shows you what you still need to revise.

They told me to mind my own business...

... so I minded my business, my history, my maths, my geography. Making and using mind maps will make your revision really effective (and *deep breath* enjoyable...) so grab your compass and go exploring.

Making Flow Charts

Flow charts are the next big thing. The talk of the town. Everyone's mad about them, haven't you heard? Don't just take my word for it though, read on and see for yourself... (gotcha, they're all my words too.)

Flow Charts Take Topics Step By Step

1) Flow charts are a type of diagram that show a process from beginning to end.
2) They organise information clearly — you can use both words and images to show what happens when.
3) It's tempting to spend ages making your flow charts look perfect but as long as they're clear and easy to use, they don't need to be fancy.

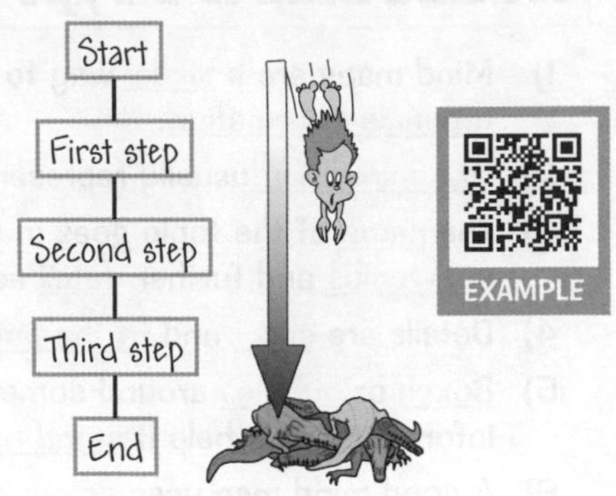

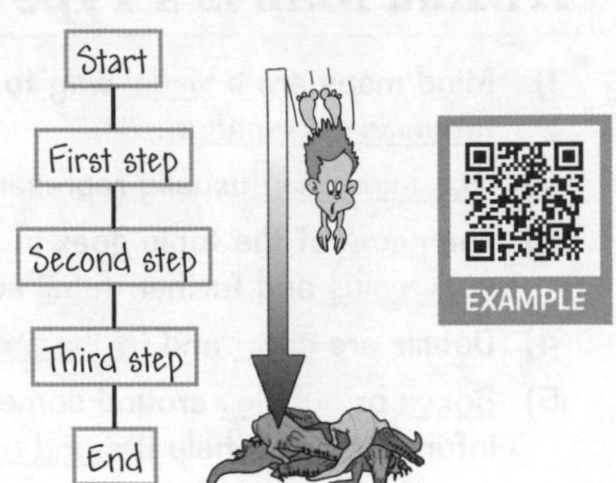

Start at the Start

1) It might sound obvious, but order is really important in flow charts.
2) Write the first step in the process at the top of the page and work downwards.
3) Flow charts highlight the main steps in a process, but if it helps, you can add key points about the different steps to jog your memory — keep them short and concise though.

They're Useful for Lots of Subjects

Flow charts show how different stages or events are linked together, so they're useful for subjects that include sequences or processes.

Here are a few examples of when you might use them:

- Business Studies — to show the different stages within a supply chain.
- History — a timeline of the events that led to the Great Depression.
- Chemistry — to set out the steps of a practical experiment.
- Geography — to present the different stages of erosion.
- Biology — to show how food passes through the digestive system.

Um, I think you missed a step...

Don't stress about it — just go with the flow...

Flow charts are a great way to mix your revision up and keep it engaging. Using the same techniques all the time is snoring (snore + boring, come on... keep up) and it's much harder to make information stick in your mind.

Using Flash Cards

Flash cards are one of the simplest, but most effective, revision tools. You might not be able to play solitaire or snap with them, but with a little patience, they'll help you bridge any gaps and get to you to número uno.

Flash Cards Are a Great Revision Tool

1) Flash cards are small cards with a question or prompt on one side, and the answer or information on the other side.
2) They're a great way to test yourself and find gaps in your knowledge.
3) Flash cards are useful for learning things like:
   - important dates in History
   - language vocabulary
   - key words and definitions
   - labelled diagrams

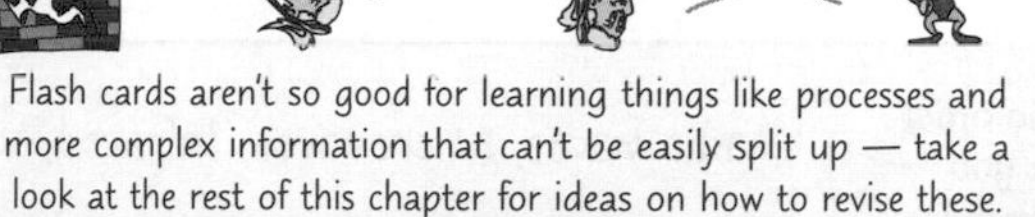

Flash cards aren't so good for learning things like processes and more complex information that can't be easily split up — take a look at the rest of this chapter for ideas on how to revise these.

4) There are lots of flash cards available online but it's a good idea to make your own. Working through your notes and picking out information is part of the process of revision.

Another great way to use flash cards is by filling one side with example questions about a topic, and the other side with the answers. This can be useful after you've revised a topic and want to test yourself on it. (I hear CGP do a pretty awesome range of question cards...)

Use Them to Test Yourself

Here are a few top tips on how to use your flash cards effectively:

Say your answers out loud — this forces you to answer the questions properly.

Test yourself until you get them all correct — make a pile of any cards you get wrong and go over them until you know them all.

Make sure you test yourself both ways — e.g. you need to know vocab translations from English to French and French to English.

Ask someone else to test you — it removes the temptation to check the other side yourself before answering.

Flash cards — lighting the way to revision success...

Flash cards are so useful because they're pocket-sized — you can take them anywhere and test yourself on the go, really making the most of any time away from your desk without having to lug all your books around.

Memory Techniques

Trying to revise without memory techniques is a bit like an arrow with no end — totally pointless...

A Mnemonic is a Memory Device

1) A mnemonic is a way of remembering facts or information in a certain order.
2) The first letters of the words you need to know become the first letters of a sentence, song or rhyme — e.g. 'Richard Of York Gave Battle In Vain' to remember the colours of the rainbow.
3) A mnemonic can be anything, as long as it makes sense to you. However, funny or rude mnemonics tend to be easier to remember.
4) This example shows you a mnemonic to help you remember the electromagnetic spectrum in order of frequency:

This is the order of waves you need to know...

Radio waves, Microwaves, Infrared, Visible light, Ultraviolet, X-rays, Gamma rays

Raccoons May Injure Very Unfortunate EX-Golfers

... this is a mnemonic sentence you could learn.

Memory Journeys Link Information to Certain Places

A memory journey is a way of linking information with landmarks on a journey. As you walk through the journey in your mind, you'll pass by all the information you need, in the correct order. Here's how to get started making one:

1) Write down the key points you need to learn.
2) Choose a journey you know well and pick your landmarks. Pick as many landmarks as the number of key points for the topic. Jot them down.
3) Assign the key points to the landmarks in order.
4) Then, make links between them. This is the fun part! Use your imagination — the wackier the link, the more memorable it is.
5) Practise walking the journey in your mind, learning the information as you go.

It might take a while to get used to this technique but it can be really useful for recalling lots of information quickly.

Memory journeys are useful for learning all sorts of things, for example, processes in Science or sequences of events in History.

Now if only I could remember where I put my notes...

Make sure you plan each memory journey carefully and go over it until you don't make any mistakes. Keep it simple or you might confuse yourself — you don't want to get distracted by remembering unnecessary details.

More Revision Tips

Don't panic about what other people are doing — do what works for you. Be a revision warrior not a worrier. Face your revision head on and be proactive. Repeat after me: I can do this. I can do this...

Revise With a Friend

If you can't see your friend in person, you could revise together over a call.

1) Test each other on different topics, e.g. using flash cards.
2) Try speaking for a minute on a topic, then get your friend to ask you questions on it.
3) Come up with funny pictures or stories to help you remember information. Get creative!

- Revising with a friend can be useful, but it's best not to do it all the time — it can be distracting and it's important to do your own revision too.
- Don't chat while you're revising. Take regular breaks, as you would if you were revising alone and save your chatting for then.

Say It Out Loud

Saying things out loud is a great way to engage with topics — it stops you skimming over details. You could incorporate this into your revision by using these ideas:

- Record yourself reading the key points of a topic and then listen to the recording regularly. Say the points out loud as you listen to them.
- Change the lyrics to some of your favourite songs to be about topics you need to remember — challenge your friends to do the same and share them.

Exercise Your Mind and Your Body

Incorporating exercise into your revision routine can really pay off because exercise stimulates your brain. There are lots of different ways of doing it, for example:

- To help with language revision, you could hit a tennis ball against a wall, reciting a different part of the verb table every time it bounces.
- Play catch with a family member and say a fact about a topic or the next step in a sequence when the ball comes to you.

My revision top tip? Um...it's on the tip of my tongue...

Treat this section like a delicious pick-and-mix of techniques — dive in and give them a try. You know you want to.

How Teachers Will Assess You

However you feel about the idea of your teachers determining your GCSE grades, remember that they just want to help you do your best. When deciding on a grade, they'll use a range of evidence — let's go...

Teachers Can Use Different Methods To Assess You

With formal exams out the window this year, teachers can use a mixture of different ways to assess you, including:

- Questions from the exam board — These could be a series of exam-style questions for the topics you've studied (see p.3).
- Mock exams — Tests that are meant to simulate a real exam (see below).
- Class tests — Tests set by your teacher. The format of these can vary (see below).
- Essays — A long piece of analysis that you'll write about a topic (see p.32-33).
- Non-exam assessments — These will vary depending on your subject (see p.28).

You Might Have Mock Exams

1) You may have already done mock exams this year. If you have, don't think they're a wasted effort now that exams have been cancelled — in fact, they're one piece of evidence in the bag that your teacher can use.
2) If you've already done a mock exam and have a reason why you think it shouldn't be used to inform your final grade, e.g. you were ill, then you should speak to your teacher.
3) If you have mock exams coming up, there are things you can do to prepare, such as past papers (see page 30) and looking at the exam specifications.
4) Even though there aren't official exams this year, it's still important to take any mocks seriously, as your teacher can use them when choosing your grade.

Take Class Tests Seriously

1. Class tests are a good way to see how well you know specific topics.
2. You should take these seriously, as they could count towards your grade and they'll help you to monitor your progress.
3. Try to keep up with your work so you're not forced to cram before any class tests.

How Teachers Will Assess You

Teachers Can Also Use Class Work

1) Teachers can use your contributions throughout the course to inform your grade.
2) Not that you should need encouraging, but it's a good idea to make a good impression in lessons:

- Make an effort to contribute to discussions.
- Ask and answer questions about topics that you cover.
- Make sure you do your fair share of work in group activities.
- Meet deadlines for all work (except in exceptional circumstances).

Don't Put Too Much Pressure On One Piece of Work

1) With all these methods, it might feel like you're constantly being assessed, but no single piece of work will determine your grade on its own.
2) Try not to let the fact that your work is being assessed put extra pressure on you. Your teachers know you and what you're capable of, so just try your best.
3) If you don't do as well as you wanted to in one assessment, just remember that it's only one piece of the puzzle. You'll be able to show what you can do next time.

Teachers Will Take Into Account Disruptions

1) Your teachers will be very aware that this year has been less than ideal for learning.
2) They'll be able to take any personal circumstances that you tell them about into consideration when you're assessed.
3) Talk to your teachers if you have any concerns about how you're coping both in and out of school.
4) If you need to catch up on a topic that you missed because of the pandemic, your teachers will be able to give you advice on what you need to know.

If you're going through a difficult time outside of school, make sure you look after your mental health, particularly while you're studying. See p.15 for who to talk to if you're struggling.

My assessment kept making fun of me — it was a mock exam...

It's always important to try your best in any assessment you're given, but even more so this year. Not only is every test a chance for you to see how you're getting on, but they can also be used to help decide your grade.

Non-Exam Assessments

Non-exam assessments are exactly what they seem — methods to test your skills that aren't exams, such as coursework, portfolios and performances. Here's some information about how they'll be used this year.

You Might Need To Do Non-Exam Assessments

1) Some subjects normally use non-exam assessments alongside exams to determine part of a GCSE grade, e.g. you might be asked to do an investigation.
2) If your subject usually requires a non-exam assessment, you might still be expected to do it in some form (and may have even completed it already).

If you're unable to complete any of your non-exam assessments due to exceptional circumstances, this will be taken into account by your teacher.

Art And Design Will Be Assessed Using Your Portfolio

1. Like in normal years, Art and Design GCSE grades will be determined by the work shown in a portfolio.
2. You should set aside time in your study plan to work on your portfolio (see p.53-55).
3. If there are materials you don't have access to that will impact the completion of your portfolio, speak to your teacher to see how they can help.
4. If your circumstances mean you can't complete your portfolio in its entirety, you'll be marked on the work you have completed.

Group Performances Might Be Different

1) Subjects such as Drama and Music usually have a group performance that counts towards your grade.
2) Circumstances this year might mean a group performance isn't possible.
3) However, you might still be expected to produce a performance of some sort to be assessed on.
4) You should speak to your teachers to see what they expect from you.

Preparing for Non-Exam Assessments

Some subjects have been hit harder than others by the changes to GCSEs, so it makes sense to draw special attention to these. Even if you don't study these subjects, it's definitely worth looking at this page.

Prepare Routines For Circus Studies

Don't just stick to one act — combine acts to show your array of talents.

Normally you'd be told which circus acts to perform, but this year you can choose. It needs to be something you can easily record, while still being impressive.

If you can juggle pineapples as well as you juggle your studying, you'll be on to a winner.

Balancing adds an element of danger to your performance. If you don't have a ball, you can balance on other things — a beam, a skateboard, your sibling's shoulders.

The more hoops you can add, the better. To really impress, keep them spinning during the written test too.

Use Suitable Equipment For Lumberjack Studies

This year you have to prepare your own equipment for the practical exam. Remember these key things:

Axe

Your axe head needs to be sharp and fastened safely to the handle to avoid errors.

Tree

Find a suitable tree to cut down — if you can't, you may have to improvise to show off your skills.

Clothing

A flannel shirt and braces are a must — without these, you may get marked down.

Design Your Own Ride For Theme Park Studies

1) **You may only have to make a model of a theme park ride, but that's a bit boring...**
2) **Instead, build your own — you'll need to apply for planning permission.**
3) **You'll also need to get a small amount of steel — 2500 tonnes should do it.**
4) **If all goes well, it should be ready for your teacher to see in around five years.**

Don't act like a clown in your assessments...

You might think this page is goofing around, but there's at least one important lesson that you can take away from here and use for your other subjects — composure, preparation and next-day delivery on steel are key.

Using Practice Exam Questions

Practice makes perfect — so give some exam-style questions a whirl to make sure you know your stuff.

Do as Many Practice Questions as You Can

1) The key to successful revision is ~~using a crystal ball~~ being well prepared — you need to know what exam-style questions look like.
2) Do as many practice questions as you can, but make sure you're only focusing your time on topics you know you'll be assessed on.
3) You could start by practising by topic. It turns out CGP have a cracking range of Exam Practice Workbooks full of topic-by-topic practice — how handy...
4) Once you've done that, try some mixed practice. You can use workbooks and practice papers, or find past papers on exam board websites.
5) Be careful using whole practice papers if you know you're only going to be tested on certain topics — you don't want to waste time answering irrelevant questions.
6) You could go through the paper and highlight the questions you're going to answer — if you want to, try reducing the amount of time you'll have for the paper based on the questions you'll skip.

If you're finding exam-style questions tricky, flick back to the previous section for some revision tips...

CGP's Top Tips for Practice

1 Don't use your notes sssh

Even if you're not doing a full practice paper, try to find somewhere quiet with no distractions, set yourself a time limit for the questions you're going to answer and don't use your revision notes to help you.

2 Use any answers or mark schemes ✓

Check what you've written against the answers or a mark scheme. Make a note of what you got wrong, how to correct it and any topics you struggled with. This will help you to avoid making similar mistakes and decide which areas you need to spend more time on.

3 Check out examiners' reports

These tell you what people struggled with, and the things that get you credit. Reading through these reports can help you see how to improve your answers.

4 Try questions again

If you have time, go back and answer any questions you struggled with again. This will help the right answer stick in your head.

5 Don't panic!!!!

If you don't get things right first time, don't worry — the idea is to get a bit better each time.

Practising questions is like washing your hair — you have to rinse and repeat...

... if you want to improve (/ have minty-fresh follicles). It's the same with jokes. I keep writing them so that one day I'll be funny. Your tests are no laughing matter though, so read the tips above and bust out a practice question.

Command Words

Stop. Sit. Read. Follow these command words and you'll soon know all about the ones in your assessments.

It's Important to Read the Question Carefully

Read the question a few times (or until you understand it).

Use the number of marks available as a guide for how long to spend on a question.

Underline or circle key phrases and command words.

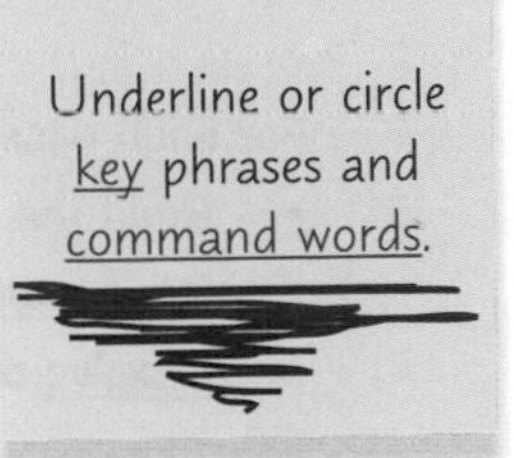

Command Words are Key — They Tell You What to Do

Common **Science** & **Maths** commands:

Command	Meaning
Describe	talk through a process or trend
Outline	state information about...
Suggest	give possible causes for...
Calculate	complete a calculation
Show	prove something is true / false
Explain	give reasons for something

Common **English** & **Humanities** commands:

Command	Meaning
Discuss	talk about key points in detail
How far do you agree?	give your opinion (and why)
How important is...	discuss the significance of...
How useful is...	weigh up the pros and cons of...
Use evidence to show...	support a view with examples
Explain	give reasons for something

EXAMPLE:

Here are some example questions that use command words.

Calculate the value of 'x'.

The command word here is 'calculate', so you need to work out a value. E.g. "x = 5". Remember to show your working if the question asks you to.

Discuss the theme of creation in *Frankenstein.*

The command word here is 'discuss', so you know this requires a longer answer that wants you to use several different opinions or bits of information.

Essay Skills

Right, it's time to look at the most useful skills in the world (apart from juggling of course). Here we go...

Take Some Time to Plan Your Answer

Planning helps you get your ideas in order, so you don't run out of things to say.

For each essay question you get:
- Read the question carefully.
- Read every text or source you need to.
- Check you know how to answer the question.

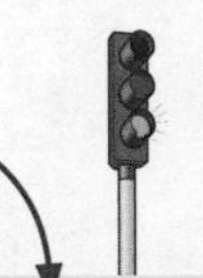

Now make a quick plan:
- Jot down your main ideas.
- Link your ideas by topic or theme.
- Outline the structure of your answer.

And remember:
- Don't spend too long planning.
- Neatly cross out your plan when you finish.

Write Well to Get Marks in Essay Questions

Structure Your Writing
- Use paragraphs to organise your points and link ideas.
- Link your paragraphs using phrases such as 'on the other hand' and 'in addition'.

You should aim to:
- Start with a short introduction.
- End with a brief summary / conclusion that clearly reminds the reader of your main argument.

Write Clearly
- Don't make your sentences too complicated.
- Check your argument is easy to understand.
- Use specific examples and precise quotes.

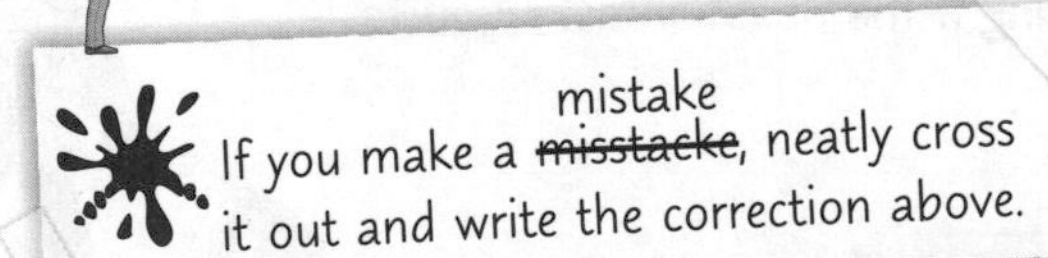

Answer the question:
- Make sure you aren't just waffling.
- Make sure everything you write is relevant.
- Keep your ideas clear and to the point.

Essay Skills

Remember That You are Writing to Impress

Standard English

Make sure you write properly:

- Avoid informal words. (Romeo's mate Mercutio) ✗
- Steer clear of slang. (The poem made me LOL) ✗
- Don't use filler words. (Pollution is, like, bad) ✗

Explaining Phrases

Explain things clearly using phrases like:

- this signifies that...
- this highlights...
- this suggests that...
- furthermore...

These will keep your answers easy to follow.

Linking Words

Link ideas and points with words such as:

- however
- in contrast
- similarly
- alternatively

They will make your answer flow nicely.

Don't Forget to Check Your SPaG

It's important to use correct Spelling, Punctuation and Grammar (SPaG) — your work will be difficult to understand if there are lots of errors.

Recipe for Perfect SPaG:

1) Avoid common spelling mistakes (e.g. mixing up 'there' and 'their').
2) Use punctuation properly — remember to check it's all correct.
3) Don't change tenses by mistake — it's confusing and won't make sense.
4) Watch out for double negatives — avoid them in your essays.
5) Start a new paragraph for a new point — don't just write in one block of text.
6) Leave time to quickly check your answers. Take 5 minutes to fix any silly mistakes.

If you want to really master spelling, punctuation and grammar, take a peek at CGP's SPaG range.

All this talk of SPaG should help you pasta tests...

Writing clearly and having good SPaG is really important for essay questions. If you don't tick those boxes, then you aren't making it as easy as possible to understand your answers — and you won't get the credit you deserve.

Weird Questions

Every so often, tests might hit you with something strange (like a fish). Don't fear though — help is here...

You Might Need to Tackle an Unusual Question

Oh no — you've flicked through your questions and seen one that looks totally unfamiliar...

1. Don't Panic → 2. Read it carefully → 3. Think it through (It's probably just asking you to apply something you do know, but in a new way.)

EXAMPLE:

Sometimes Maths problems might be set in a real-life (wordy) context.
This means you have to work out what you need to do before you can do the maths:

Underlining the information you need can help.

> Elon buys apples in crates of 50 apples. Each crate costs £22.50.
> He presses 3 crates of apples every weekday (Mon-Fri) and 2 crates per day at the weekend.
> How much will it cost Elon to buy enough crates of apples to keep pressing them for 5 weeks?

Use what you've underlined to create the correct calculations for your answer:

Number of crates needed for 1 week = (3 x 5) + (2 x 2) = 19
Number of crates needed for 5 weeks = 19 x 5 = 95
Total cost of every crate needed = 95 x £22.50 = £2137.50

Be Prepared for Tricky (But Predictable) Questions

If you know certain types of questions are bound to come up, you can be ready for them.

History: Using Sources

In History, you can get questions which ask you to decide how useful a source is — these can be tricky. It might help to ask yourself:

Does any info make the source more / less reliable?

Consider:
- Who wrote it
- Who they wrote it for
- Why they wrote it

Does the source match what you know about the topic?

- Compare what you know about the topic with the information in the source.
- If they don't match, think about why.

Does the source tell the full story?

- Consider whether the source leaves out key information.
- The source may be unreliable if the writer is deliberately trying to hide something.

Weird Questions

English Literature: Unseen Poetry

You might still need to do unseen poetry — if you do, remember to:

1) READ the poem — work out what it's about.
2) IDENTIFY the poem's message — think about why the poet wrote it.
3) EXPLORE emotions and feelings — consider the poem's mood.
4) PICK OUT literary techniques — explain their effect and use quotes.
5) INCLUDE your thoughts — think about how the poem made you feel.

Science: Calculation Questions

**A good chunk of marks are usually available for calculation questions.
If you find maths daunting, these things can help:**

Show Your Working Out → You may get marks for it and it helps you spot silly errors.

Check Your Answer → Make sure your answer seems sensible.

Read Tables / Graphs Carefully → Double check you've used the correct figures.

Geography: Case Studies

Think of Case Studies as detailed examples. You could be asked to evaluate, explain or suggest things based on your knowledge. When answering Case Study questions:

Avoid general answers that could be about anywhere.

Use clear and specific details (e.g. dates, place names, events).

Answer the question — don't just write out every fact you know.

EXAMPLE:

There was an earthquake in Italy that caused lots of damage.

In 2009, over 300 people in L'Aquila (Italy) died following an earthquake which left more than 60,000 people homeless.

Do dogs have eyebrows, or do some eyebrows just have legs?

Don't let these pages panic you too much — it's unlikely you'll get asked anything *really* weird in your assessments. It's a good idea to be prepared for all the tricky things that might come up though, just in case...

Taking Your Tests

To make sure you're in tip-top test-slamming condition, here are some last-minute things you can do.

Get Organised the Night Before

Spend time the night before making sure you're prepared:

1) Eat a balanced meal (see p.18).
2) Get anything you're taking with you ready to go.
3) Double check when your test is.
4) Do something relaxing or some gentle exercise.
5) You could read over some notes, but don't cram all night.
6) Try to get a good night's sleep (see p.18).

Check with your school what you need to bring.

Kit Checklist

- Multiple pens and pencils ✓
- A rubber and sharpener ✓
- A pencil case ✓
- A water bottle ✓
- Subject-specific stationery, e.g. ruler, calculator etc. ✓

Get Ready at a Sensible Time

1) On days with a test, make sure you're not rushing to get to school. It's hard to keep a clear head if you're flustered or rushing late, so allow plenty of time in the morning.
2) Eat a healthy breakfast with a glass of water and fruit.
3) If you have time, look over your notes at any key definitions, formulas, facts and quotes. Don't revise anything new though — save your energy.

Focus on What You're Doing During the Test

1) Read each question carefully.
2) Read each question carefully — seriously, you might miss something if you rush.
3) Answer every question that you need to — and don't answer any that you don't.
4) If you're not sure of an answer, make an educated guess.

5) Judge how long to spend on a question based on how many marks it's worth.
6) Make sure you have time to check your answers.
7) Don't get distracted by what others are doing.

Dealing with FTPs (Frequent Test Panics)

If you can't answer a question...
Move on to the next question and come back to it later.

If you're running out of time...
Answer questions which require short answers to pick up as many marks as possible.

If you realise halfway through a question that you've got it wrong...
Cross out what you've done and write your new answer beneath it.

Taking Your Tests

Try to Relax After Each Test

1) It's natural to feel worried after doing a test or assessment, particularly this year — but remember that your teacher will take into account the circumstances you're under.
2) However it goes, try to learn from the experience for future tests too. For example:

If you ran out of time, think about how you could manage your time differently.

If you felt tired, consider how to improve your routine the night before.

If you panicked, try practising some relaxation techniques that you can use to stay calm in future tests.

3) Tests are tiring — find some time to relax as soon as you're able to.
4) If you're feeling frustrated or anxious, doing some exercise could help.
5) If you have another test later the same day or the next day:

- You may want to have a quick look over some notes.
- But be sure to have a break between looking at any notes and the test itself.
- Don't forget any final preparations (see previous page).

6) When you've had a break, put your notes for the test you've done away — this can act as a physical reminder of what you've achieved already.

~~Scream and Dance Around~~ Unwind After Your Last Test

1) When all your tests and assessments are over, store your notes out of sight (but don't throw them away).
2) Be proud of what you've achieved — it's particularly impressive under the circumstances.
3) Plan a treat to celebrate all your hard work.

To fill the study-shaped hole in my life, I memorised cereal ingredients...

Try to put tests to the back of your mind and not worry about results day. Enjoy the well-earned free time you have, maybe by learning a new party trick — wholegrain wheat, sugar, barley, salt, iron, vitamin B6...

Maths

Additional tips coming your way, divided into different subjects. The handy tips on these pages will give you warm, fuzzy feelings for Maths that will only multiply, so you'll never want to subtract it from your life.

Practice is the Best Way to Improve

1) The best way to learn and get better at maths is by doing practice questions.
2) Start by practising questions on specific topics to get to know them.
3) Then practise doing a mixture of topics — this will help you identify weak areas.

Remember Formulas with Flash Cards

1) Flash cards are good for learning formulas.
2) Write a prompt on one side of the card, and the formula on the other side (see p.23 on how to use flash cards).

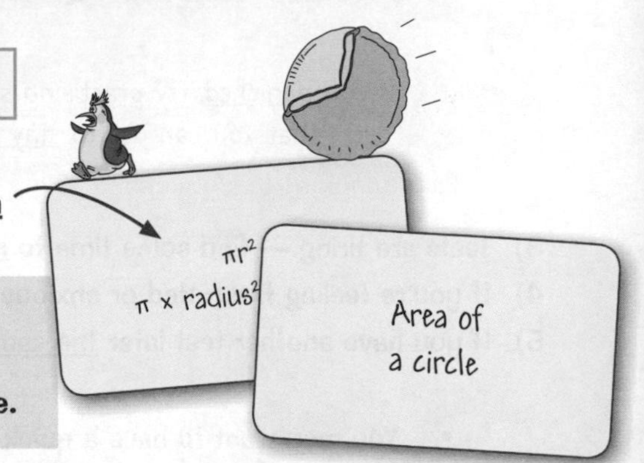

Check with your teacher to see which formulas you need to learn, whether you'll be given a formula sheet and if there are any formulas you really, *really* need to memorise.

Get to Know Your Calculator

It's important to know how to use your calculator for tricky problems.

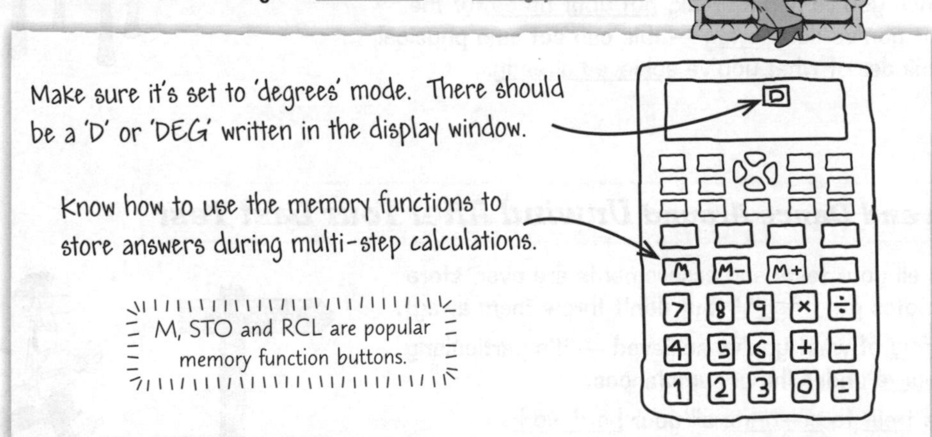

Use memory functions to avoid rounding too early

If you get an answer with lots of decimal places during a multi-step question, use the memory function. You can then use that number for the next step instead of rounding, which may affect your final answer.

Maths

Understand What a Question is Asking

1) Know what each command word wants you to do.
2) If you're given a number of marks, use it as a guide to how much time you should spend on a question.
3) Show your working out — you might get some credit on the question, even if your answer is wrong.
4) Answer in the correct units, or to the correct number of significant figures or decimal places.

Command Words

- Write down/state — give a brief answer
- Calculate/find/solve — show your working out
- Explain — give a written reason for your answer

EXAMPLE:

Take a look at this question. There are plenty of ways to avoid answering the question incorrectly.

> **11** The formula for the period, T seconds, of a pendulum of length l metres is given by:
>
> $$T = 2\pi\sqrt{\frac{l}{g}}$$
>
> At the equator, $g = 9.78$ m/s^2.
>
> (a) Find the period of a pendulum, of length 30 cm, at the Equator.
> Give your answer to 3 significant figures.
>
> $T =$ .... seconds
> [2]

You're given a length in centimetres, but the formula uses lengths in metres. You need to convert 30 cm into metres.

The command word is 'find' so you need to show your working out.

Make sure you round your final answer to 3 significant figures.

You need to answer the question in seconds.

Check Your Answer Makes Sense

1) Make sure your answer is sensible — a person can't be 22 m tall.
2) Check for silly mistakes — 3 × 3 is not 6.
3) If you've solved an equation, put the answer back into the equation to see if it's correct.
4) Expand factorised brackets to check they give you the original expression.

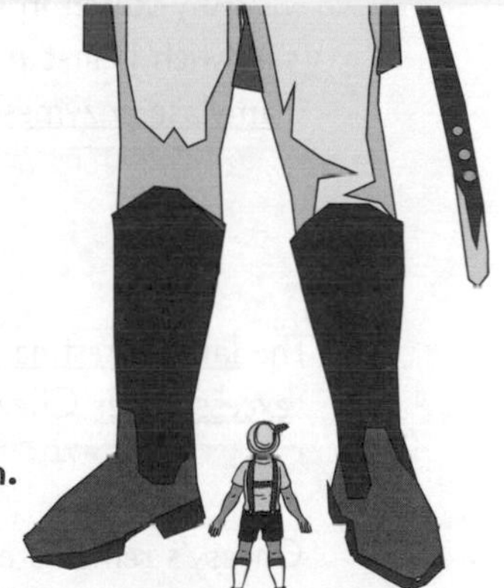

I always check every page I write for chicken silly mistakes...

One of the (many) great things about GCSE Maths is that most questions have definite answers, meaning you can check whether you've got the right answer. Maths gets a bad rap sometimes, but it's actually very generous.

Science

You and science probably have quite the chemistry now, so you'll be glad to hear there are things you can do together to help with your learning. Not that you two need an excuse to spend time with each other...

Match Pairs to Learn Key Terms

1) Write key terms and their definitions on separate pairs of cards. Then jumble and sort the pairs.
2) When you can sort them all, try recalling the definitions based on the term only.

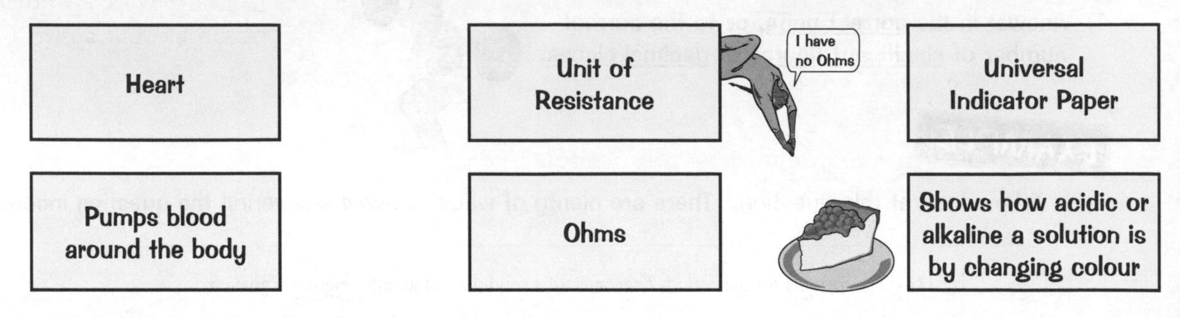

Learn Scientific Processes With Storyboarding

To help you understand processes with many steps, you could create stories.

EXAMPLE:

You could storyboard the digestive system like this:

You can't describe processes in an informal way like this when answering a real question — you need to use scientific language and terminology.

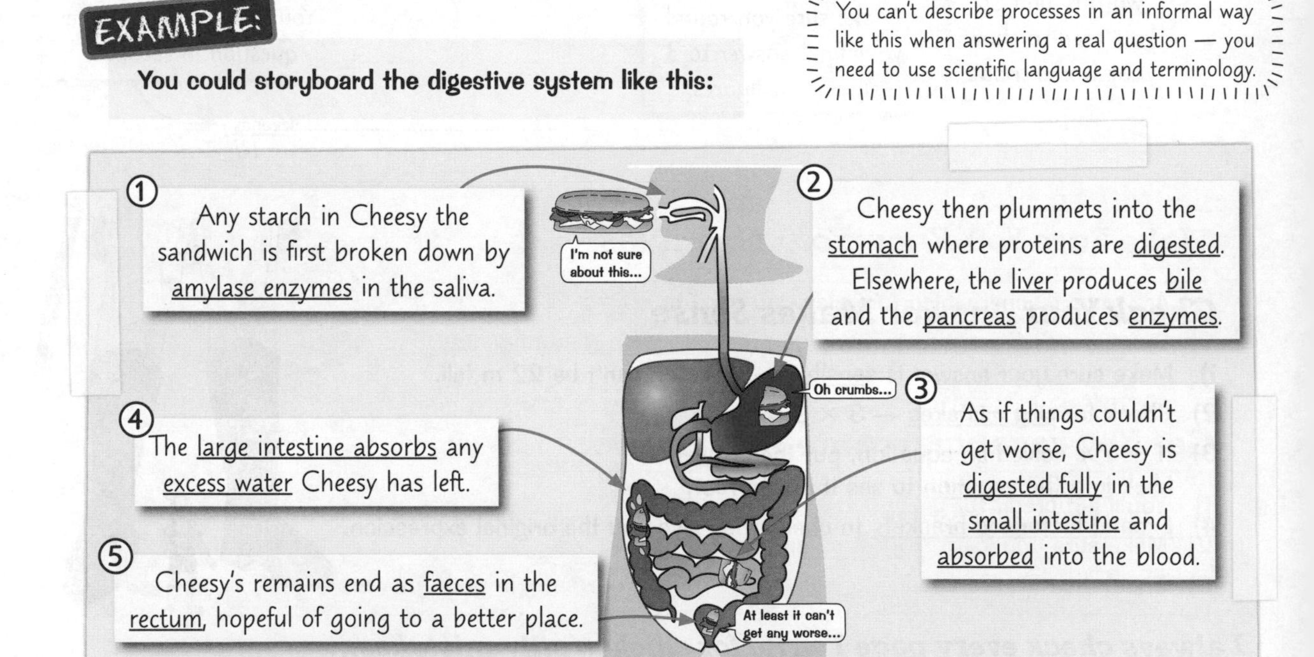

Science

Get to Grips with Practical Skills

Even if you're not conducting any practicals yourself, you may have to answer questions about practicals:

1) Learn the names of equipment and how to improve the quality of the data obtained.
2) Be familiar with how to record data — e.g. don't include units in the main body of a table.
3) Practise drawing graphs, using a ruler and sharp pencil for accuracy.

Take a look at this practical skills question.

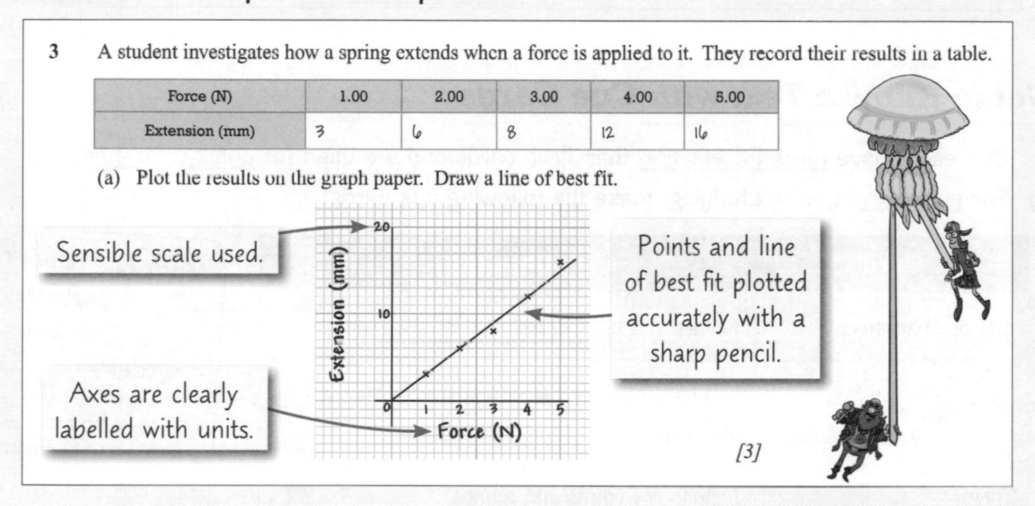

3 A student investigates how a spring extends when a force is applied to it. They record their results in a table.

Force (N)	1.00	2.00	3.00	4.00	5.00
Extension (mm)	3	6	8	12	16

(a) Plot the results on the graph paper. Draw a line of best fit.

[3]

Make Sure You Know Your Formulas

1) Ask your teacher which formulas you need to learn.
2) Practise using every formula so you can use them all confidently.

Get Key Vocabulary into Your Answers

1) You'll get credit for using correct terminology.
2) Make sure you learn key words and their meaning.
3) Check that you've used relevant scientific terms correctly in your answers.

I don't trust atoms — I hear they make everything up...

But you won't when you're really prepared — here's a pretty useful formula to start you off: GO_2D $PL4N_2ING$.

English Literature

Fun fact — pneumonoultramicroscopicsilicovolcanoconiosis is the longest word you'll find in a dictionary. Fortunately, learning about English Literature isn't nearly as daunting as trying to write that word.

Organise Your Work for Each Text

1) Make sure you know which texts you're going to be tested on — you might not be assessed on all the texts you've already read for your GCSE course.
2) For each text you'll be tested on, write a short summary of what it's about.
3) For longer texts, note down important plot points or passages too.
4) This will help you to remember key information about each text.

Close enough...

Get to Know a Text with Cue Cards

1) Cue cards have more information than flash cards and are used for quick reference.
2) For every text you're studying, make the following cue cards:

Card	Details
List of Characters	Names and brief description of who's who.
Main Characters	List each main character's characteristics and a quote that sums them up.
Themes	Include key points and quotes.
Context and Audience	When and why the text was written, and how the context affects the text.
Writer's language	Language techniques used by the writer and quotes that show these being used.

Much Ado About Nothing
Beatrice:
- Witty/Intelligent
- Outspoken
- Confident
- Loyal to Hero
- Annoyed by gender stereotypes
- Reluctant to marry

"she mocks all her wooers out of suit"

Make sure you only answer questions on the texts you've studied.

A Christmas Carol
Theme — Family:
- Happiness — Belle's family full of **"joy, and gratitude"**.
- Loneliness — Scrooge was **"a solitary child"**.
- Scrooge's change — becomes a **"second father"** to Tiny Tim.

3) You can use cue cards in different ways:
   - Read a set of cards for a different text frequently, e.g. each day.
   - Put the cards somewhere you'll see them, e.g. on the fridge.
   - Ask someone at home to test you using your cards.

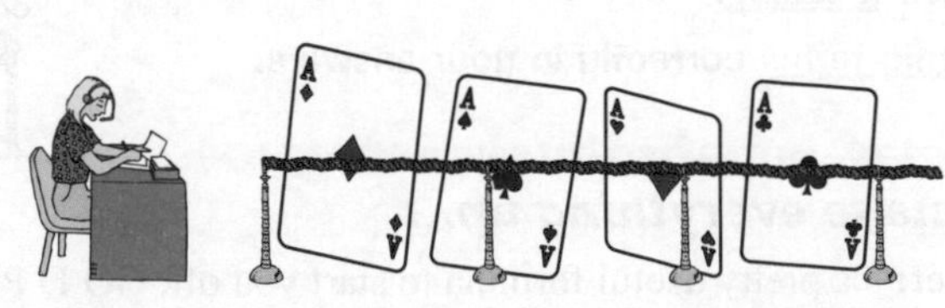

English Language

Language is a super word — there aren't many words that end in 'uage'. Jejune is also a great word — it means uninteresting, but this page isn't jejune. It's anti-jejune, jejuneless, jejune-free. I could go on...*

Read (and do) Practice Questions

1) The way you'll be assessed might be different this year, so it's important to find out from your teacher what question types you might be assessed on.
2) Practise planning and writing answers out in full.
3) Also practise analysing unseen texts. Make sure you:

- READ the text carefully.
- UNDERLINE key words as you read the text.
- NOTE the writer's view after reading the text.

4) You should show the following skills when answering questions:

- Write critically and clearly
- "Use quotes to back up your points"
- Analyse language, form and structure
- Show you understand how context affects the text

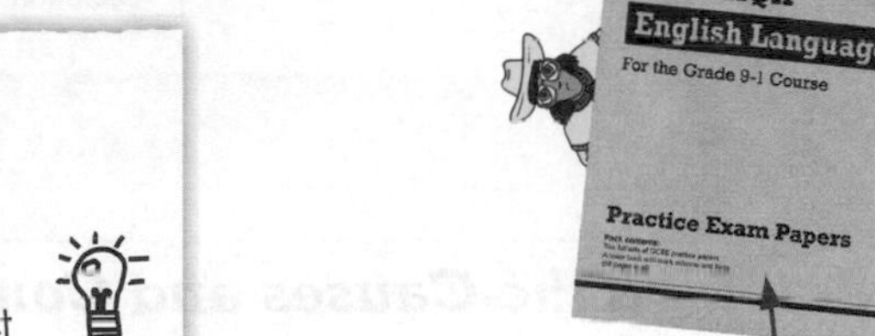

5) You can find past papers for your exam board online (CGP do some practice papers too. Just sayin'...)

You Might be Assessed on Your Creative Writing

1) You should practise writing both fiction and non-fiction texts.
2) Make sure you also practise writing for different audiences and purposes. For example:

Write an article for a broadsheet newspaper in which you explain your point of view.	Write a speech for a debate at your school in which you argue for or against a statement.

3) Aim to make your writing interesting, accurate and well organised.
4) If possible, get someone to read your writing so you can get feedback.

Look at past papers for writing prompts to get your creative juices bubbling.

**This page is jemarch, jeapril, jemay, but absolutely not jejune...*

Make sure you're clear on the different ways Language and Literature will be assessed. You don't want to spend weeks practising writing *A Christmas Carol* fan fiction when you won't get asked to write one for either subject.

History

My teacher told me everything in GCSE History was in the past, so imagine my surprise when I found out that the assessment was actually in the future. Speaking of the future, I spy two helpful pages of tips in yours...

Use Timelines to Learn Events

1) When answering questions, you need to be able to say when events happened.
2) Make a timeline to help you learn the order of events, e.g. for battles or new laws.
3) Draw pictures on your timeline as a way to remember key events.

This is a timeline of the events leading to Hitler becoming Führer.

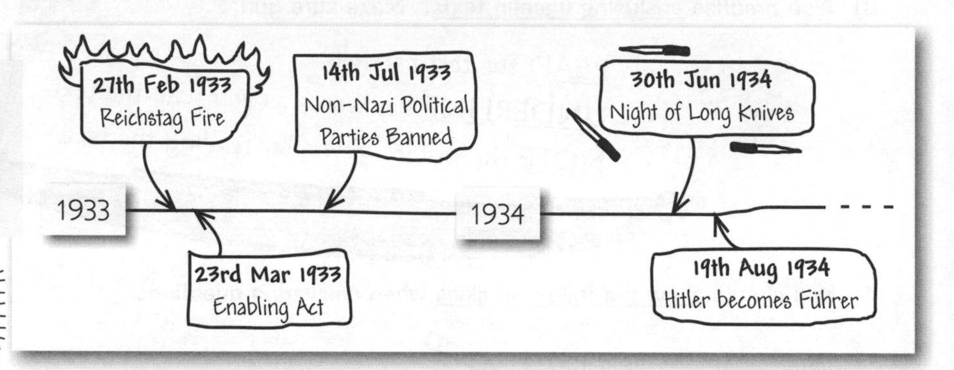

Learn what happened in each event too.

Understand the Causes and Consequences of Events

It's not enough to know what happened for each topic — you should know why the event happened (the causes) and what happened after the event (the consequences).

Causes

- Think about which causes were more important/less important, e.g. reasons for a war.
- Consider the short-term and long-term causes.
- Think about a range of different causes for an event, e.g. social, political, financial.

Consequences

- Write down two or three things that changed because of an event.
- Rank these things in order of importance.
- Decide if the event was mainly good or bad.

1923 German Hyperinflation

Farmers sold goods for more money

Good

Papiermark became worthless

Rebellions broke out

Bad

History

Tailor Your Answer to the Question

1) Double check the topic and dates mentioned in a question.
2) If the question asks about a date range, focus your answer on those years.
3) Be sure to answer the question — don't just write everything you know about a topic.
4) Back up each point you make with facts and details. For example:

> Life was hard for African Americans in 1920s America because segregation was widespread and many could not vote.

The only answer Hank won't tailor is fashion from last year...

There Might be Different Question Types

1) Some questions in your assessment may require longer answers than others.
2) Questions worth a few marks only need a short answer.
3) Spend most of your time on questions that you need to write an essay for.

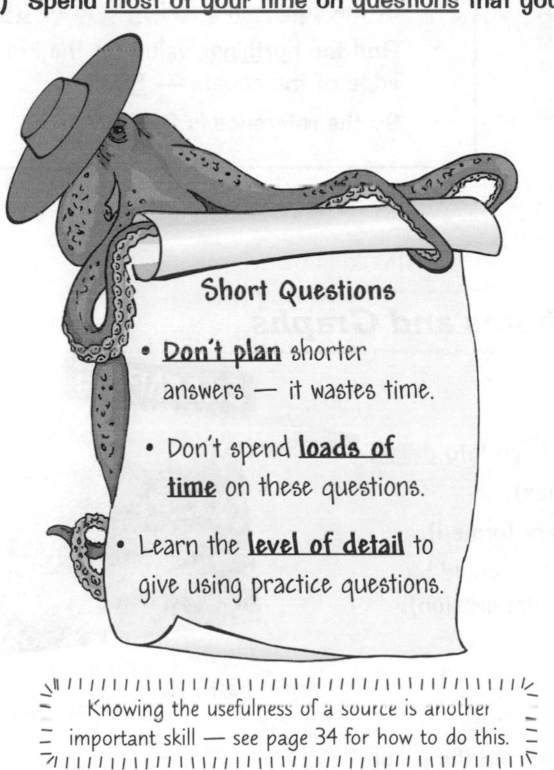

Short Questions

- **Don't plan** shorter answers — it wastes time.
- Don't spend **loads of time** on these questions.
- Learn the **level of detail** to give using practice questions.

Long Essay Questions

- Write a **quick plan** before you write your long answers.
- Talk about **both sides** of an argument.
- In your **conclusion**, say which side of the argument is **strongest** and **why**.

Knowing the usefulness of a source is another important skill — see page 34 for how to do this.

Double agents are like History essays — they talk about both sides...

Unlike spies though, your long essay answers shouldn't be subtle about mentioning both sides. Remember to include facts to back up any points you make and keep your answer focused on the topic and time period stated.

Geography

You're in for a world of fun now — these pages will help 'Geog' your memory before you tackle any tests.

Make Sure Your Map Skills are Strong

1) You might need to know about Ordnance Survey® maps for your test. You should know how to use eastings and northings to reference squares on a map grid:
   - Eastings increase as you move east.
   - Northings increase as you move north.
   - Always write the eastings value first.
2) You should also be able to work out the distance between two places on a map:
   - Use a ruler to measure the distance between the places in centimetres.
   - Compare your measurement to the scale to get the distance in kilometres.

EXAMPLE:

Give the four figure reference of the smiley face.

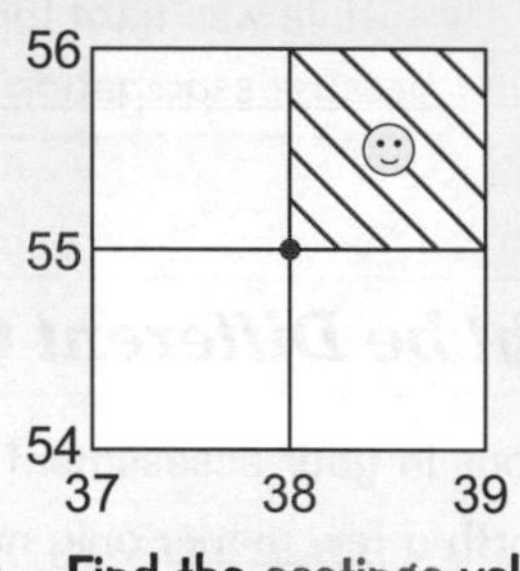

Four figure grid references give you a square.

- Find the eastings value for the left edge of the square the smiley is in — 38.
- Find the northings value for the bottom edge of the square — 55.
- So the reference is 3855.

You Need to be Able to Discuss Photos and Graphs

Picking Apart Pictures

When describing a photo like the one on the right, go into detail:
- Name features (e.g. beaches, cliffs and arches).
- Describe specific features (e.g. how they were formed).

You might even be asked to describe processes that could be taking place in the photo (e.g. weathering or coastal erosion).

EXAMPLE:

Figure 1, a photo showing part of the Dorset coast in the UK.

Grappling with Graphs

- When describing graphs, always refer to data from the graph.
- Remember — a line of best fit shows a trend.
- Know that scatter graphs can show +ve or -ve correlation.

Geography

Be Prepared to Answer Longer Questions

Some questions in a Geography test may ask you to write a bit more.

Use ADELE to remind you about what to include in your longer answers:

A — Accurate knowledge (facts and figures)
D — Detailed Understanding (make it clear that you 'get it')
E — Examples (include specific, relevant examples)
L — Links (use conjunctions, e.g. however, additionally, although...)
E — Evaluations (give your opinion or judgement)

Some longer answers may ask you to talk about Case Studies — see page 35 for how to manage these.

Don't Forget to Use the Right Terminology

1) Make sure you use the correct terminology and technical terms for processes.
2) It's important that you understand what key terms mean so that you can use them correctly in your answers.

Be Familiar with Maths

1) Some questions might ask you to use maths, so you need to know how to figure out:

- MODE = MOST common
- MEDIAN = MIDDLE value (when values are in order of size)
- MEAN = TOTAL of items ÷ NUMBER of items
- RANGE = DIFFERENCE between highest and lowest

2) You also need to be able to calculate percentages and percentage change:

- PERCENTAGE = (Part of Sample ÷ Total Sample) × 100
- PERCENTAGE CHANGE = $\frac{\text{Final value - original value}}{\text{original value}} \times 100$

What is central to understanding Geography? The letter 'r'...

Geography tests you on a wide range of skills, so you'll have to become familiar with all sorts in order to do your best in your assessments. It's not all bad though — chances are you'll get plenty of nice pictures to look at...

Languages

Whatever comes your way in your assessments, these handy tips will help you out. You're welcome...

Get To Know Your Vocab

Learning the vocab is really important, but you don't need to spend hours staring at vocabulary lists:

Turn your house into a dictionary
- Label items in your home such as rooms or furniture.

Make flash cards
- Write the vocab on one side of the card and the English word or a picture on the other side.
- Ask someone to test you.

Use your voice
- Say the vocab out loud to yourself or a friend.
- You could record yourself and then play it back.

Use Verb Tables to Learn Different Tenses

Verb tables are a great way to easily see the verb endings for different tenses.

Subject	Past	Present	Future
I			
You (sing)			
He/She/It			
We			
You (pl)			
They			

Make a table for each type of verb ending — pick a regular verb for each ending to use as an example.

Create blank copies of your table and test yourself by filling them out from memory — you could practise using different verbs.

Focus on Specific Verbs

1) **Make a note of verbs you struggle to remember or often get wrong — irregular verbs tend to be the trickiest.**
2) **Make a verb table for each irregular verb. Use a different colour for the conjugations you find difficult, e.g. the verb 'dar' in Spanish:**
3) **Practise writing sentences using these verbs in different tenses — check the conjugations using your verb tables.**

Subject	Present
I	doy
You (sing)	das
He/She/It	da
We	damos
You (pl)	dais
They	dan

Languages

Hone Your Translation Skills

1) Being able to translate between English and the language you're studying is really important — you'll have to translate passages into English and translate English into the other language.
2) Here are some top tips for translation:

- Make sure your translations sound natural.
- Translate the text one sentence at a time rather than one word at a time.
- Watch out for different tenses.
- If you come across a word you don't recognise, don't panic:

Think about whether the word is similar to any other words you know in English or another language — it could have a similar meaning.

Think about the context — you might be able to guess the word's meaning based on the rest of the sentence.

If you're still unsure, make a sensible guess rather than leaving a blank space.

Practise Useful Phrases

It's important to learn topic vocab, but there are more general words and phrases that will help you too. Spend some time making and learning lists of different expressions that will allow you to answer questions more easily:

Opinion words: e.g. 'I think...', 'I believe...', 'Personally...'.

Time expressions: e.g. 'tomorrow', 'last year', 'next weekend'.

Conjunctions: e.g. 'therefore', 'but', 'because', 'consequently'.

Comparisons: e.g. 'more than', 'less than', 'the same as', 'on the other hand', 'in contrast'.

I used the past, present and future in my language test — it was intense...

Nothing else needs to be though — "bye bye tense, hello calm". Don't worry if there's a word or phrase you don't recognise straight away — just see if you can work it out using the handy tips above. As always, it's my pleasure.

Chocolate Studies

If you're not aware of GCSE Chocolate Studies, you'll probably think this page is nonsense. However, if you are studying this completely real and totally not made-up subject, sink your teeth into some sweet knowledge.

Blind Taste Test to Learn Chocolate Types

1) You'll need to know about different types of chocolate.
2) Get pieces of the main chocolate types — dark, milk and white.
3) Close your eyes and pick a piece of chocolate at random. Eat and enjoy.
4) Guess the chocolate — ask someone to tell you if you got it correct.

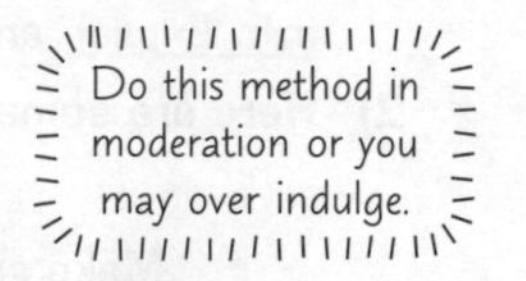

Don't show preference to one type of chocolate

Your teacher will have their favourite type of chocolate, so you need to discuss them all equally in any essay question.

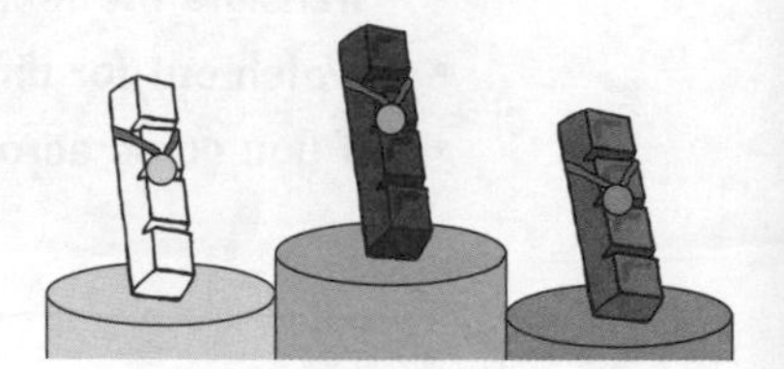

Know Important Chocolate Quotes

Chuck Alot, Chocolate Philosopher — 'Better to have had chocolate and lost, than to have never had chocolate at all.'

Botanist, Dame Cara Mel — 'A people without the knowledge of chocolate is like a tree without roots.'

Life Guru, Candice Cane — 'The journey of a thousand chocolates begins with one bite.'

Learn These Uses for Chocolate

Religious Studies

You're unlikely to be asked to write an answer evaluating the ethical statement 'It's always good to study', but it's something I'm sure we can agree on. Continue your path to study enlightenment with this page.

Learn Beliefs and Practices in Detail

When studying religious beliefs and practices, get used to doing these three things:

1. Explain what the belief means.
2. Link the belief to a teaching or quote.
3. Explain why the belief is significant to religious people today.

EXAMPLE:

Here's how you might summarise a religious belief:

Belief → Christians believe humans are made in God's image.

What it means → Christians believe that God made all humans like Him, so everyone is important.

Quote / Teaching → In Genesis 1:26, God said "Let us make mankind in our image".

Significance Today → Christians may support charities which tackle injustice or inequality, because they believe that every person is valuable and should be treated with respect.

Debate Ethical Questions

1) **With a family member or a friend, decide on an ethical statement, e.g. 'The death penalty is always wrong'.**
2) **Toss a coin to decide who is in favour and who is against the statement.**
3) **Take two minutes each to put forward established arguments for or against it.**
4) **Turn it into a game — give points for examples, religious teachings and key terms.**

Learn to Tackle Essay Questions

1) **Any essay answers you write should give balanced viewpoints and refer to religion.**
2) **Remember that there are often differences of opinion within a religion, e.g. Protestants and Catholics hold different viewpoints on different topics.**
3) **Use precise examples, e.g. 'An example of natural evil is natural disasters, such as hurricane Katrina.'**
4) **Essays should always have a conclusion, where you can give your opinion on what you've discussed.**

I've tried provoking fish into arguments — they never take debate...

You'll end up studying a lot of serious ethical topics — try debating something light-hearted for a laugh, like 'cows are the best farm animal to take ice fishing' (I'd hate to argue against that one...).

Business Studies

I had this great idea to set up a website where you can order loads of stuff to your door with just a click of a button — I'd call it 'Rainforest'. I couldn't get a financial backer though — something about competitors...

Learn Key Business Definitions

Make sure you're familiar with the different command words that come up so you know what you're being asked to do.

1) Learn business definitions, particularly for any multiple-choice questions.
2) Longer questions may also give credit for knowledge of key terms.
3) The best way to learn these definitions is using flash cards (see p.23).

Read Case Studies Carefully

1) For questions that are based on case study information or on data, make sure you use evidence from the case study or data set as well as your knowledge of Business in your answer.
2) Before you get started, read the case study and any data all the way through. Then read the whole question carefully and make sure you've understood what you're being asked to do.
3) If you're asked to evaluate something, make sure you produce a balanced argument that discusses the positives and negatives, even if you then come to a conclusion supporting one side.

THIS JUST IN

YOU SHOULD TAKE AN INTEREST IN BUSINESS NEWS

- CASE STUDIES ARE BASED ON REAL BUSINESS CHALLENGES
- WATCHING BUSINESS NEWS WILL MAKE YOU AWARE OF KEY ISSUES
- YOU'LL LEARN REAL-LIFE EXAMPLES

Practise Your Maths Skills

1) Maths crops up a fair bit — you need to be able to do the following:

   - Use maths in a business context, e.g. calculating the average rate of return.
   - Interpret data and draw graphs, e.g. reading or plotting a total revenue line.
   - Use formulas, e.g. to calculate the break-even point.

2) Remember to show your workings and any formulas used — this may get you credit.
3) Make sure you give your answer to the number of decimal places that the question asks for.

Don't delay — turn your business studies into busyness studies...

Hurrah, it's the last page of the section. Reward yourself with some exciting Business Studies practice questions.

Make A Study Planner

The last part of this book is a study planner (all paper-based I'm afraid — we had a bit of a struggle finding a personal assistant who would fit). It'll help you get organised and as ready as can be for all of your studying.

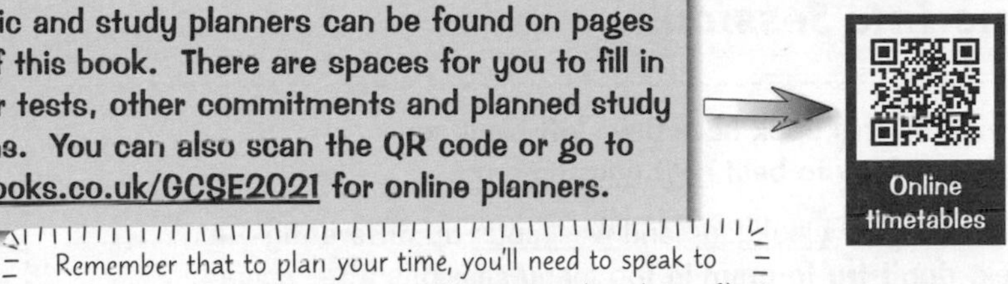

Your topic and study planners can be found on pages 60-85 of this book. There are spaces for you to fill in all of your tests, other commitments and planned study sessions. You can also scan the QR code or go to cgpbooks.co.uk/GCSE2021 for online planners.

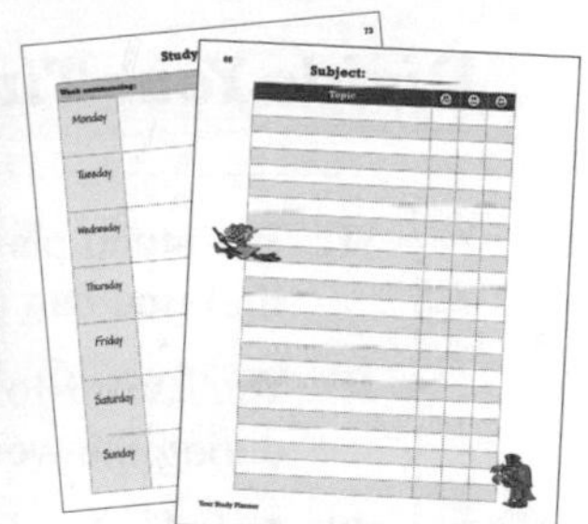

Remember that to plan your time, you'll need to speak to your teachers to find out what you'll be assessed on (see p.6).

Write Down all of your Important Dates

- When you get given a deadline or dates for tests, e.g. for an exam-style assessment, class test or non-exam assessment, add it to the list of important dates on pages 58-59.
- You should refer to this list regularly, so you can see at-a-glance what you've got coming up. It'll help you stay focused.

EXAMPLE:

Important Dates

Subject	Type of Work	Date	Time
Maths	Assessment	May 10th (Mon)	9:00
Biology — Cells	Topic Test	May 12th (Wed)	15:00
English — Frankenstein	Essay Deadline	May 17th (Mon)	-
English	Assessment	May 18th (Tues)	14:00
Chemistry	Assessment	May 21st (Fri)	11:00

Break each Subject Down into Topics

- Fill in the Topic Planners on pages 60-70 for each of your subjects (see below).
- Use these planners to list the topics your teacher has said that you could be assessed on.
- Put a tick in the column that shows how happy you feel with each topic. Update the table as you feel more confident.
- Try to do as much practice as you can so that you're as happy as possible with each topic.

Don't worry if there are some topics where you missed lessons — see pages 10-12 for the best ways to catch up and work independently.

Biology

Topic	☹	☺	😉
Cells	✓		
Microscopy	✓		
Cell Differentiation and Specialisation	✓	✓	
Stem Cells	✓		

Make A Study Planner

It might seem like a lot of organisation that isn't getting any of the subject stuff in your head, but good planning now will save all sorts of time later — time that can be spent, y'know, studying and revising.

Divide Your Time Into Sessions

1) The study planners in this book have been left blank so that you can choose how to best split your time up.
2) You'll want to divide your weekdays and weekends up differently — during the week, don't try to cram in too many sessions after school.
3) To help you divide your day into sessions, think about:
   - what time of day you work best
   - when you get up and go to bed
   - how long you'll study each day
   - fitting in sensible breaks
4) It's up to you how long each session is, but try having several shorter sessions rather than one long session on a topic or subject.

A good rule of thumb is to break for 10 minutes every hour — either in one chunk, or split into two 5-minute breaks.

Fill In Your Commitments

You can't study all the time — you need to make time to relax (see p.17 for advice).

1) Go through your study planner, adding in the time for things like:
   - hobbies and regular exercise
   - birthdays
   - calls with friends and family
   - picnics
2) It's also a good idea to keep some time free in your plan in case something unexpected comes up — there may be things that you can't plan for, so if there are a few gaps, it'll make it easy to adapt.

It's important to have breaks and treats to look forward to (see page 8).

EXAMPLE:

This planner uses 50-minute revision sessions, with 10-minute breaks after each one.

Start at a sensible time, based on your daily routine, e.g. after school on weekdays.

Week commencing:					
Monday	16:00-16:50	17:00-17:50	18:00-18:50	19:00-19:50	20:00-20:50 Running
Tuesday	16:00-16:50	17:00-17:50	18:00-18:50	19:00-19:50	20:00-20:50

Add your commitments and activities.

Make A Study Planner

Add Your Subjects

1) Decide how much time you'll need to spend on each subject by thinking about:
   - what your teachers recommend focusing on
   - which you find the hardest
   - which have more content
   - which you will be tested on first
2) Add your subjects into the planner, thinking about the deadlines you have.
3) Try your best to allow enough time for each and space them out over the time you have (see p.56 for more on this).

Colour-coding your planner by subject makes it clearer.

EXAMPLE:

Week commencing:					
Monday	16:00-16:50 Biology	17:00-17:50 Maths	18:00-18:50	19:00-19:50 History	20:00-20:50 Running
Tuesday	16:00-16:50 English Lit	17:00-17:50 Geography	18:00-18:50 French	19:00-19:50	20:00-20:50 History

Add Your Topics

1) For each subject, look at the topics in your topic planner — think about which you should prioritise (like you did with your subjects) and add those first.
2) Aim to include topics more than once to give you a chance to revise them thoroughly and more concisely each time. You should also allow yourself time to do practice exam questions (see p.30).
3) Make sure you leave plenty of space for all of your topics — you might want to write in pencil to start with.

Cover topics where you have gaps in your knowledge first, then move on to revising topics you've already learnt.

You don't have to do this step straight away — you might prefer to fill in the topics at the start of each week once you know how you're getting on. Don't be afraid to edit your planner as you go along, depending on what's going well and what you feel less confident with. Just try to leave enough time to cover every topic in enough detail.

Week commencing:					
Monday	16:00-16:50 Biology -Cell Biology	17:00-17:50 Maths -Algebra	18:00-18:50	19:00-19:50 History -Practice Exam Q	20:00-20:50 Running
Tuesday	16:00-16:50 English -Poetry	17:00-17:50 Geography -Practice Exam Q	18:00-18:50 French -Past tenses	19:00-19:50	20:00-20:50 History -Elizabeth I

Add topic detail under each subject.

Space It Out and Mix It Up

Think About S p a c i n g As You Plan

Revisiting a topic several times, with gaps in between, is more effective than trying to study it all in one go. It helps the information sink in better so that it's easier to remember.

① Space out your work on a topic across the time you have available — try to leave enough time to go over a topic more than once.

② Don't be tempted to cram a whole subject into a day — it won't be as effective.

③ It's okay to cover different topics from the same subject on the same day, just make sure you don't do it too often — keep your studying varied to keep your brain engaged.

Make Sure You Mix Your Subjects Up

1) Include a good mix of subjects every day — don't cover all of your languages or sciences in one go.
2) Split your work on each subject into short, focused chunks spread over different days and several weeks — leaving a gap between them will help you retain the information better.
3) It's not a good idea to spend a week revising just Maths and then a week on English — the information just won't stay in your brain in the long-term.

Week commencing:

Monday	Biology	Maths		History	Running	
Tuesday	English Lit	Geography	French		History	
Wednesday	Maths	Cycle		English Lit	Physics	
Thursday	←	Call Martha	→	Chemistry	History	
Friday	French		Physics	English Lang	Maths	
Saturday	History	Running	Spanish		Maths	Physics
Sunday	Gaming	Chemistry	English Lang		French	English Lit

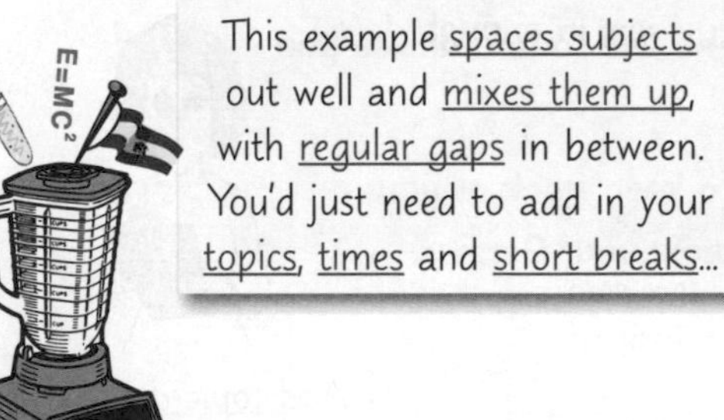
This example spaces subjects out well and mixes them up, with regular gaps in between. You'd just need to add in your topics, times and short breaks...

My planners are so good, people call me a revisionary...

Oh come on, that was a good one. Speaking of good ones, you should have a pretty gosh darn good planner in front of you by this point. Just a couple more things before you go...

Checking Your Study Planner

Hey, you, I see you about to skip this page — before you race off excitedly to start using your shiny new planner, it's a good idea to spend a few minutes checking you haven't anything important.

Check Your Planner

1) Run through the checklist below and compare each point with your planner.
2) If there's anything missing, go back and fill it in.

1. Have you included the deadlines you know about? ☑
2. Have you added in topics for at least the first few weeks? ☑
3. Have you double-checked the dates? ☑
4. Does the planner cover a mixture of subjects each day? ☑
5. Have you planned in regular breaks? ☑
6. Have you left time for things you enjoy doing? ☑
7. Have you left a few gaps to change things if you need to? ☑

Stick To Your Planner — but be Flexible

It's all well and good making yourself a great planner, but it's no use to you unless you follow it.

1) **Use your study planner alongside your topic planners to keep track of your progress.**
2) **Don't be afraid to adapt the plan as you go — if you know your German tense endings better than you thought but need to spend more time on quadratic equations, just swap things around as you need to.**
3) **If something doesn't go to plan one day, don't panic — Just fit any missed studying into the gaps you've left in the planner and carry on.**

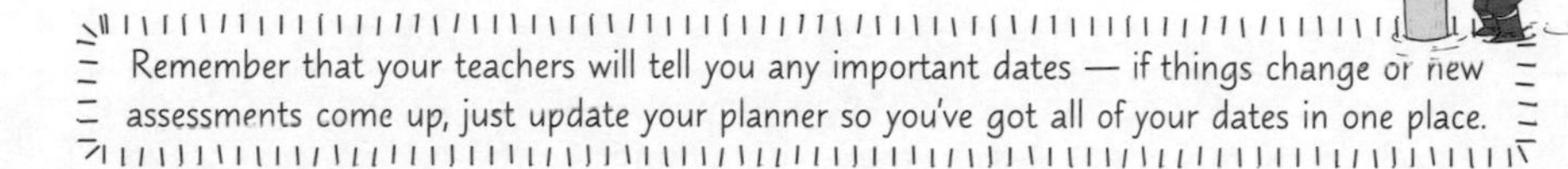

Important Dates

Subject	Type of Work	Date	Time

Important Dates

Subject	Type of Work	Date	Time

We've started this topic planner for you, you lucky thing, so just grab your notes and finish it off.

Subject: Maths

Topic			
Multiples, Factors & Primes			
Fractions			
Decimals			
Percentages			

Subject: ______________

Topic	☹	😐	☺

Subject: ________________

Topic			

Subject: ____________

Topic			

Subject: ______________

Topic			

Subject: ___________________

Topic	☹	🙂	😉

Subject: ______________

Topic	☹	🙂	😉

Subject: ____________

Topic			

Subject: ____________

Topic			

Subject: ______________

Topic			

Subject: ___________________

Topic	☹	🙂	😉

The Perfect Cup of Tea

The making and drinking of tea are important life skills. It's not something that's likely to crop up in any of your assessments, but it is something that will make studying much easier. So here's a guide to making the perfect cuppa...

1) Choose the Right Mug

A good mug is an essential part of the tea drinking experience, but choosing the right vessel for your tea can be tricky. Here's a guide to choosing your mug:

2) Get Some Water and Boil It

For a really great brew, follow these easy step-by-step instructions:

1) First, pour some water into a kettle and switch it on. (Check it's switched on at the wall too.)
2) Let the kettle boil. While you're waiting, see what's on TV later and check your belly button for fluff. Oh, and put a tea bag in a mug.
3) Once the kettle has boiled, pour the water into the mug.
4) Mash the tea bag about a bit with a spoon. Remove the tea bag.
5) Add a splash of milk.

Note: some people may tell you to add the milk before the tea. Scientists have recently confirmed that this is nonsense.

3) Sit Back and Relax

Now this is important — once you've made your cuppa:

1) Have a quick rummage in the kitchen cupboards for a cheeky biscuit. (Custard creams are best — steer clear of any ginger biscuits — they're evil.)
2) Find your favourite armchair/beanbag. Move the cat.
3) Sit back and enjoy your mug of tea. You've earned it.

Phew — time for a brew I reckon...

It's best to ignore what other people say about making tea and follow this method. Trust me, this is the most definitive and effective method. If you don't do it this way, you'll have a shoddy drinking experience.

Study Planner

Here's an idea of how you could fill in your study planner — have a look, then turn the page and start your own.

Week commencing: 22nd March

Day				
Monday		17:00–17:50 Walk with Deja	18:00–18:50 Maths — Algebra Topic Test Revision	19:00–19:50
Tuesday	16:00–16:50 Revise for Chemistry Test	17:00–17:50 German — Translation Practice	18:00–18:50 Running	19:00–19:50
Wednesday	16:00–16:50 Art Portfolio	17:00–17:50 Call with Gran	18:00–18:50	19:00–19:50 Maths — Powers & Roots
Thursday	16:00–16:50 Bike ride	17:00–17:50 Geography — Migration Assignment	18:00–18:50 Physics — Atoms & Isotopes	19:00–19:50
Friday	16:00–16:50 English — Poetry Essay	17:00–17:50 Biology — Cell structure	18:00–18:50	19:00–19:50 Pizza Friday!

Day						
Saturday	10:00–10:50 Study Session with Greg	11:00–11:50 Biology — Diseases	12:00–12:50	13:00–13:50 Baking? *Nom...*	14:00–14:50 Chemistry — Past Paper Questions	15:00–15:50 Geography — Global Development
Sunday	10:00–10:50 English — Short Essay on Macbeth	11:00–11:50 German — Past Tense (for test on Monday)	12:00–12:50	13:00–13:50 Physics — Radioactive Decay	14:00–14:50 History — Vietnam War	

Study Planner

Week commencing:	
Monday	
Tuesday	
Wednesday	
Thursday	
Friday	
Saturday	
Sunday	

Study Planner

Week commencing:	
Monday	
Tuesday	
Wednesday	
Thursday	
Friday	
Saturday	
Sunday	

Study Planner

Week commencing:	
Monday	
Tuesday	
Wednesday	
Thursday	
Friday	
Saturday	
Sunday	

Study Planner

Week commencing:	
Monday	
Tuesday	
Wednesday	
Thursday	
Friday	
Saturday	
Sunday	

Study Planner

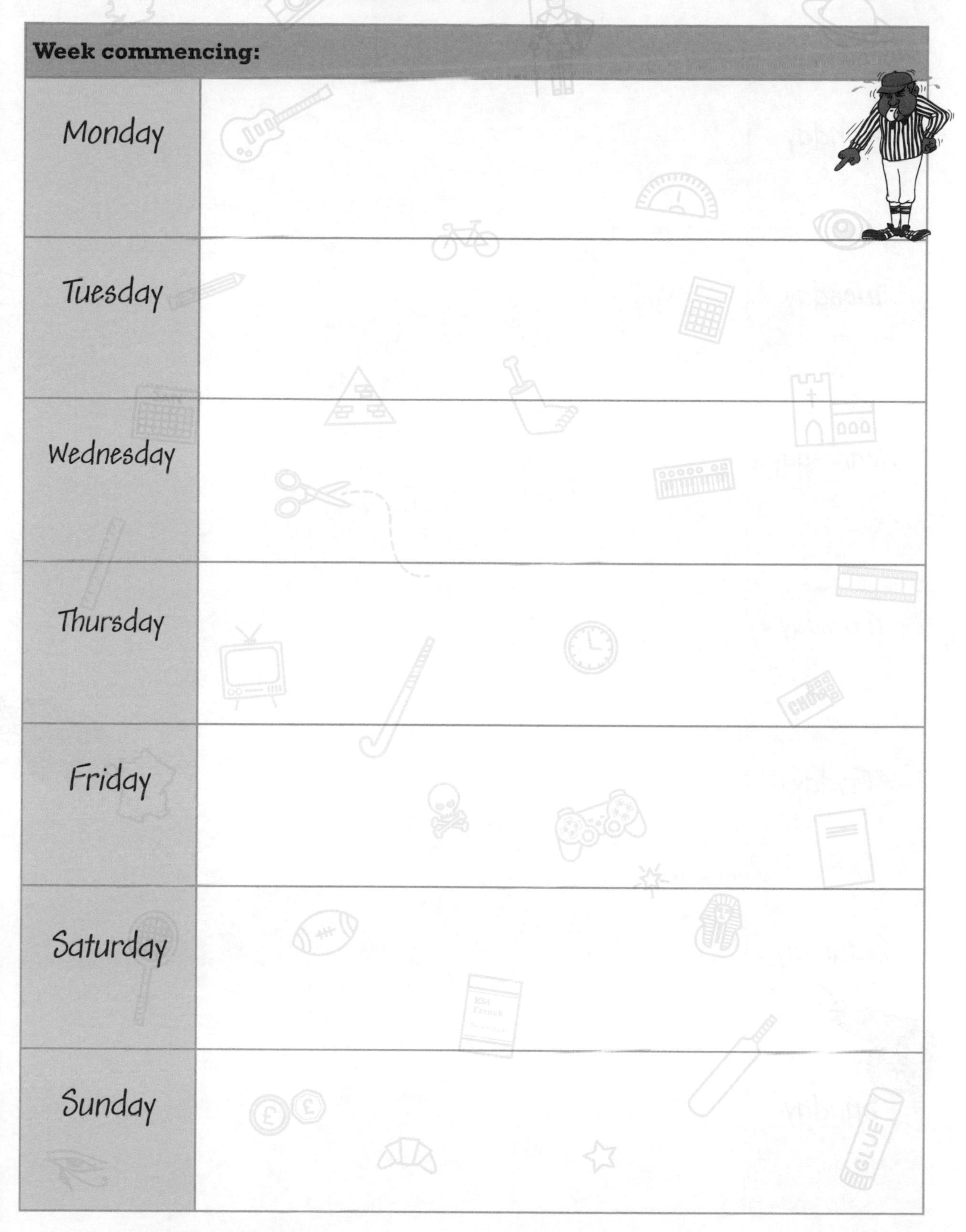

Week commencing:	
Monday	
Tuesday	
Wednesday	
Thursday	
Friday	
Saturday	
Sunday	

Study Planner

Week commencing:	
Monday	
Tuesday	
Wednesday	
Thursday	
Friday	
Saturday	
Sunday	

Study Planner

Week commencing:	
Monday	
Tuesday	
Wednesday	
Thursday	
Friday	
Saturday	
Sunday	

Study Planner

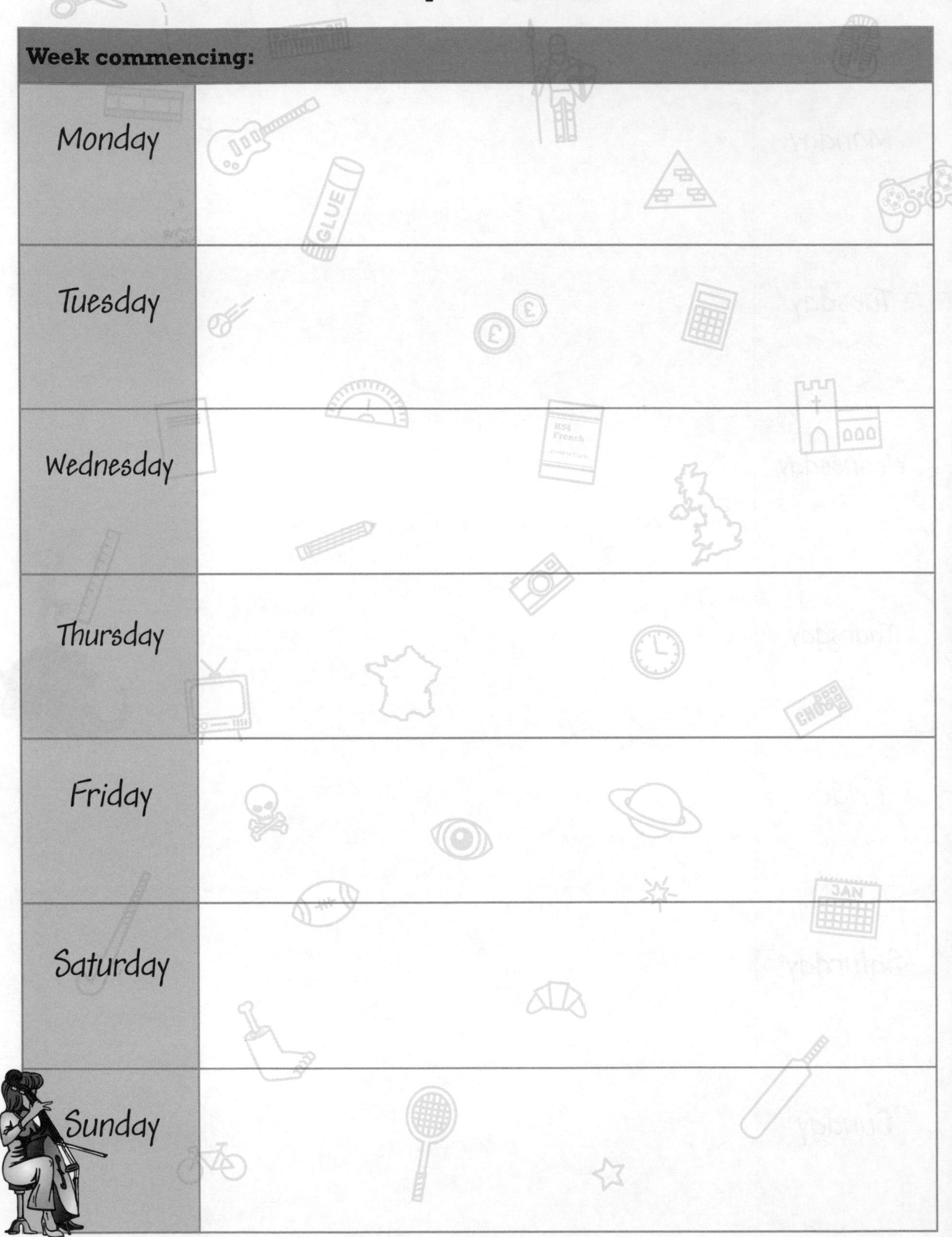

Week commencing:	
Monday	
Tuesday	
Wednesday	
Thursday	
Friday	
Saturday	
Sunday	

Study Planner

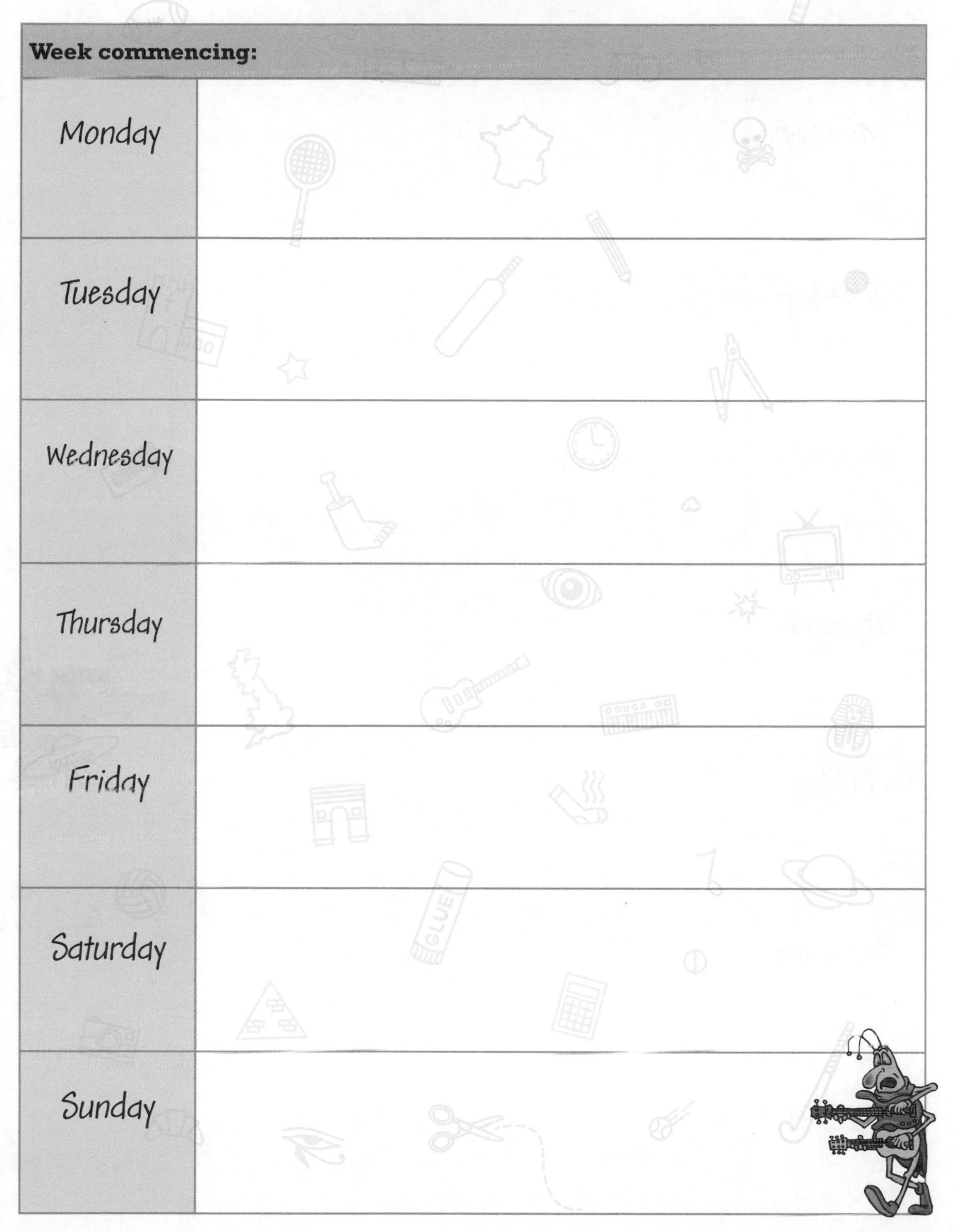

Week commencing:	
Monday	
Tuesday	
Wednesday	
Thursday	
Friday	
Saturday	
Sunday	

Study Planner

Week commencing:	
Monday	
Tuesday	
Wednesday	
Thursday	
Friday	
Saturday	
Sunday	

Study Planner

Week commencing:	
Monday	
Tuesday	
Wednesday	
Thursday	
Friday	
Saturday	
Sunday	

Study Planner

Week commencing:	
Monday	
Tuesday	
Wednesday	
Thursday	
Friday	
Saturday	
Sunday	

Study Planner

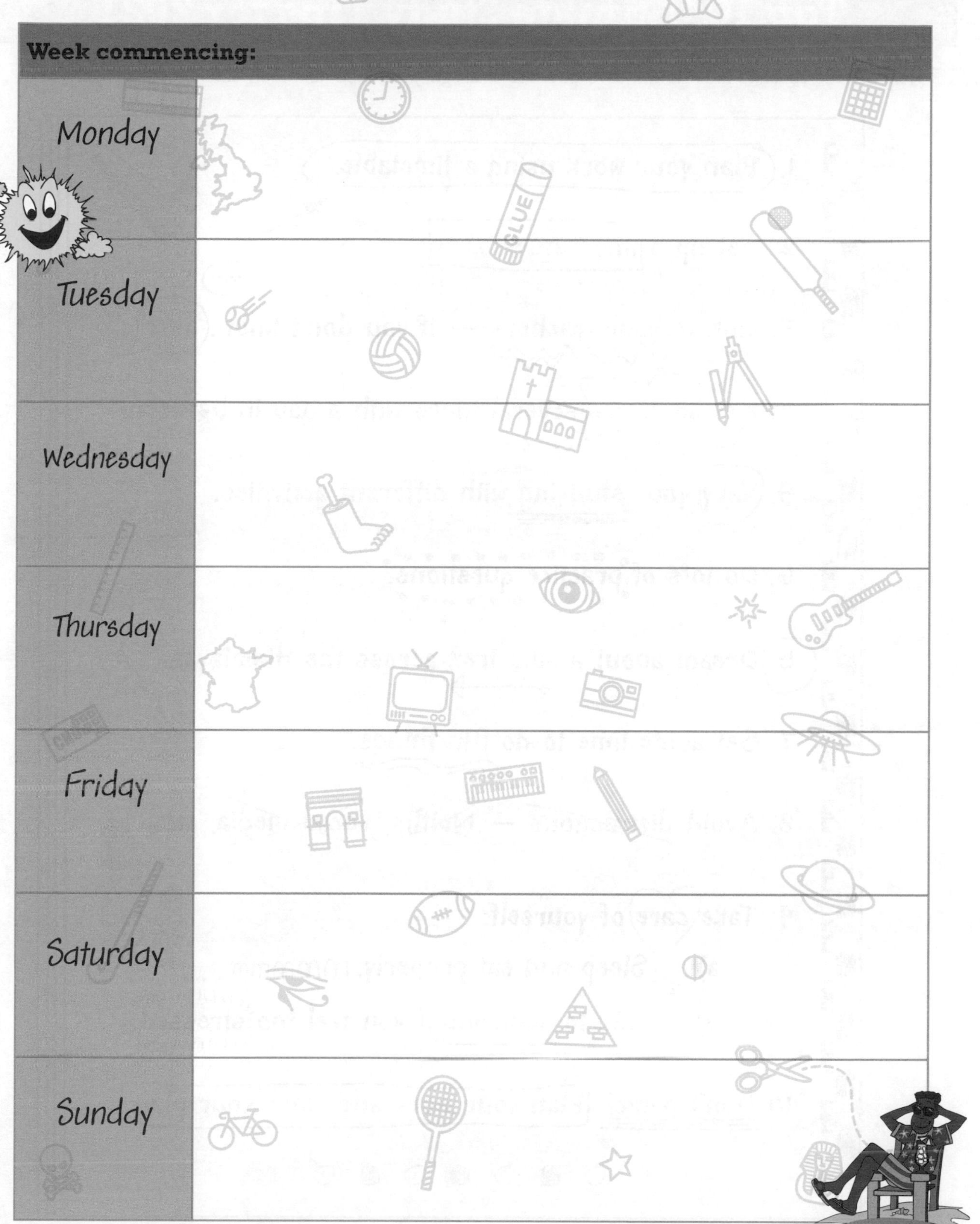

Top 10 Ultimate Study Tips for 2021

Here are the absolute must-know, save-your-life-in-a-fight-with-a-zombie-test, ultimate study tips.

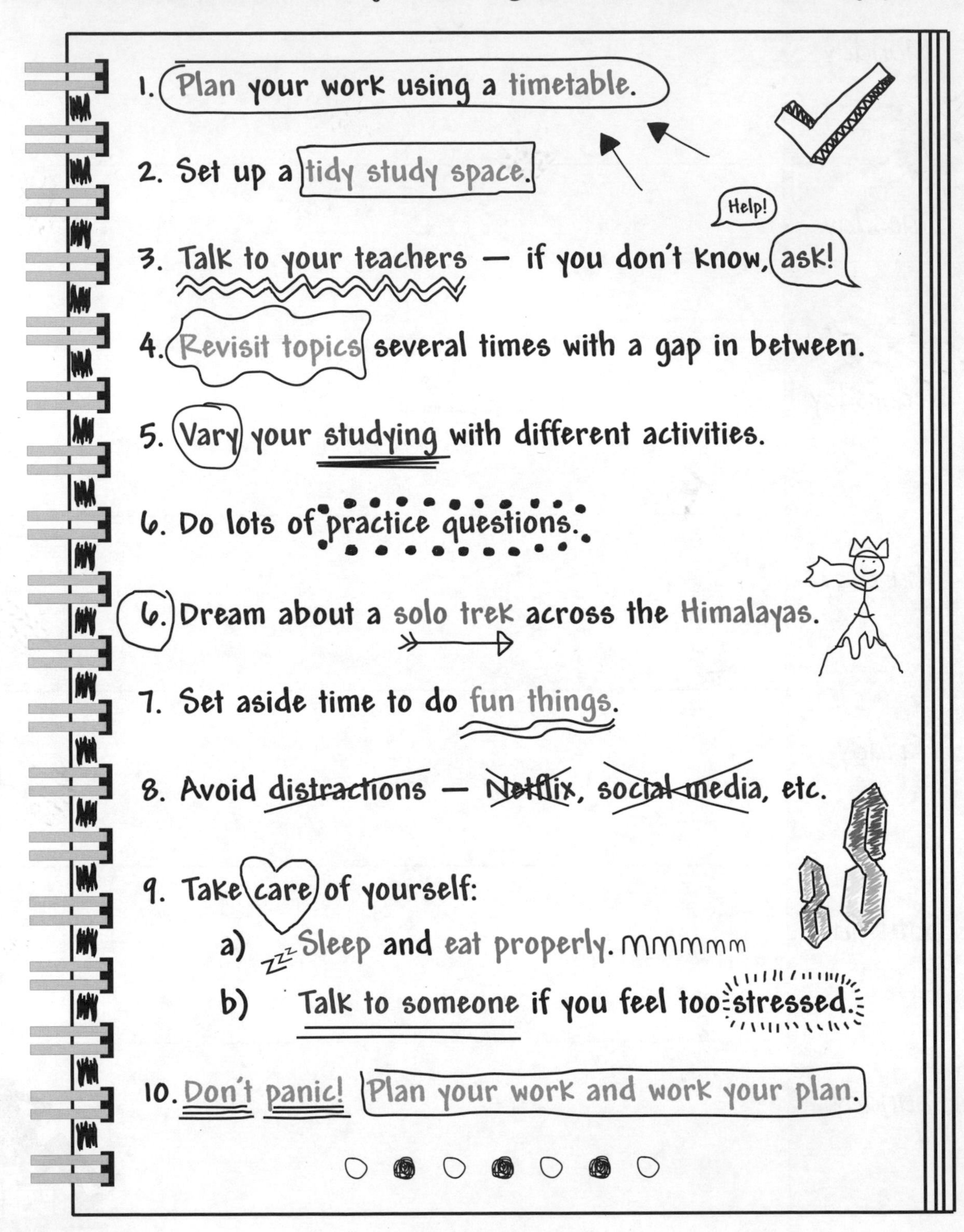